Eustace Clare Grenville Murray

**Side-Lights on English Society**

Or sketches from life. Social and satirical

Eustace Clare Grenville Murray

**Side-Lights on English Society**
*Or sketches from life. Social and satirical*

ISBN/EAN: 9783337097110

Printed in Europe, USA, Canada, Australia, Japan

Cover: Foto ©Suzi / pixelio.de

More available books at **www.hansebooks.com**

# SIDE-LIGHTS

# ON ENGLISH SOCIETY,

OR

SKETCHES FROM LIFE, SOCIAL & SATIRICAL.

BY
E. C. GRENVILLE MURRAY,
AUTHOR OF 'THE MEMBER FOR PARIS,' 'THAT ARTFUL VICAR,' ETC.

*Illustrated*
WITH NEARLY 300 ENGRAVINGS.

IN TWO VOLUMES.
VOL. I.

LONDON:
*VIZETELLY & CO., 10 SOUTHAMPTON ST., STRAND.*
1881.
[*All rights reserved.*]

TO

# THE QUEEN.

MADAM,

A threefold purpose has animated me in dedicating this book to your Majesty. In the first place, as a loyal subject, I eagerly embrace the opportunity of laying before you the tribute of my homage. In the second place, I am proud, as a man of letters, to seek for my work the notice of a Sovereign, not the least of whose titles to the gratitude of a distant posterity will be, that in her reign, and owing, in no small degree, to her fostering care, arts and letters have so flourished in this island that the Age of Victoria may challenge comparison with the Ages of Elizabeth and Anne. Thirdly, as an Englishman, I venture to submit for the consideration of the Head of our race a careful study of some of the most important aspects of English society, as at present constituted.

## DEDICATION.

A survey of the condition of the English people leaves one much to be thankful for, especially the fact that its best expression is modelled on the pure example of your Majesty's life. But if this nation is to continue to lead the vanguard of progress, and persistently to move towards the perfect ideal of a great kingdom, united under the sway of a beloved line of Princes, it is obvious that it behoves us to look the defects of our social and political system boldly in the face, neither extenuating aught, nor setting down aught in malice. An evil acknowledged is half cured; above all, in the country for which your Majesty's ancestors did so much to secure the priceless boon of liberty of thought and discussion. Much, however, remains to be done; and our very freedom, which none dare openly attack, is at this moment exposed to subtle and dangerous machinations.

Your Majesty's prerogative and the mighty influence of your august person have been steadily exercised, throughout a long and glorious reign, in support of every cause that approved itself to the best spirits of the time. Your Majesty's gracious intervention has redressed many a wrong, has given hope to the oppressed, and taught the most powerful of the earth to respect the unwritten laws of equity and honour.

That your Majesty may long be spared to be the protectress of the weak and the terror of evil-doers, and still to direct your people in the way of peace and happiness, truth and justice, religion and piety, is the fervent prayer,

MADAM,

Of your Majesty's most devoted grateful Servant
and faithful Subject,

E. C. GRENVILLE MURRAY.

# PREFACE.

SOCIETY is a many-headed thing; it is not easy to take its photograph; and perhaps a too faithful likeness would not be accepted by those who know it best as a correct portrait.

This is the difficulty. Society wears a conventional expression, and has struck a conventional attitude once and for all. Like the customers of the late Madame Rachel, she covers her face with pearl-powder and rouge, and means to be beautiful for ever. The artist must not be curious to see what lies under her enamelling. Mr. Du Maurier's clever young painter, who won renown and wealth by doing the portrait of Lady Midas, showed the way which all writers might perhaps, if they consulted their own interests, follow with most profit. But how would Hogarth have painted Lady Midas? How would her ladyship have fared at the hands of George Cruikshank, Mr. Sambourne, or Signor Pellegrini?

The writer must claim the same liberty as the artist, the more so as his works obtain a lesser publicity. The books of Fielding and Smollett—possibly Thackeray's *Book of Snobs* too—are not read by new thousands every day; but Hogarth's pictures, multiplied indefinitely by engraving, are seen constantly by millions of eyes all the world over. There are fashions in printed matter; but apparently none in pictures, which, if true to life, are admitted to an everlasting popularity. All critics cry to the artist, 'Copy Nature—avoid the lay-figure.'

Probably Society in the eighteenth century did not much relish the satire of the 'Mariage à la Mode;' and we know how George II. expressed himself about the 'March of the Guards to Finchley.' That picture is now the chief ornament of the collection at the Foundling Hospital. Is it that the Governors of the Foundling have become less loyal? No; but because the picture is recognised as a good piece of painting, throwing a valuable 'side-light' on queer manners which have now passed out of existence. And doubtless, if his Majesty's pet soldiers mended their ways, Hogarth's sermon in oils had something to do with it.

## PREFACE.

When there is a tacit understanding among public men that Government must be carried on by an organised system of falsehood, deceit, and injustice; when no official statement, however solemn and precise, can claim respect or belief; when all but the rich are driven from the judgment-seat, and hope for the orderly redress of wrongs is mocked by law-costs; when our social polity arouses serious and widespread discontents; when administration is paralysed by parliamentary insanity,—Reform is needed, and Reform is near.

It is no longer a party question; it concerns every person who can distinguish between right and wrong; and if many powerful individuals are always opposed to the public interest, sensible people should unite to detect them, and to put down their influence. But if we reward every one who ventures to lift his voice against existing abuses with ostracism; if officials who profit by notorious abuses are allowed to silence honest accusers with rattening and slanderous clamour, it is hard to see what can be done. Nepotism and patronage are at the bottom of it; and all that has been discovered about patronage shows that it is most often given for fear or money. Such facts look ugly in print; but Dapper and Capper can talk of them with perfect coolness at their clubs, and so can Flapper.

It is positively marvellous that the best talent of our land has so long remained in voluntary obscurity, and that men who have made politics the study of their lives are content to write their own degradation daily in essays and leading articles, as though the good things and honourable professions of this world were the natural heritage of dolts only. It is quite disconcerting again to think how noble a calling diplomacy might be, and to see how pitiful a thing it is. It was the business of my choice. It cost me a great deal of money to follow it; and I was ultimately hustled out of active service by a clerk who had embezzled my salary. But for seventeen years I worked at diplomacy as an ambitious lawyer drudges at the law. I loved it as a soldier loves his sword.

In a word, I believed in it. Diplomacy seemed to me that which it might and should be—a simple and peaceful method of furthering all the best and highest interests in the world. I considered it the nurse, the tutor, and guardian of commerce; the pioneer of science; the harbinger of peace, destined to banish strife and discord from the earth. I thought that it should teach nations to know and understand each other so well that disputes and misapprehensions would become impossible, and that it should be the messenger of kindness and good-will among all peoples.

I collected, with laborious care, whatever seemed to me in any way to bear upon the duties I had, or might have, to perform. No fact appeared to me too trifling, no research too minute, that gave me a clearer knowledge of things belonging to my profession. By these means I slowly accumulated some facts and useful precedents; and I spent ten years of my life in compiling a work on international law. A deceased clerk alone knows what has become of it. It was seized by his order, together with my private papers, now (1881) near three lustres since; and I have never been able to get news of them, though the Queen herself very kindly supported my application to a Secretary of State for the return of my lost property. I should say that her Majesty most graciously did so, but it was really a *kind* act; and I like to speak of it, as it is graven in my heart.

I have written these lines with all the sad and yearning love which an exile feels towards his country. I have suffered twelve years of banishment—not from any displeasure of my Sovereign, or from popular clamour, but from the resentment of an official who had grown rich and influential by the misappropriation of public money; and though he has long since gone to render his account before a tribunal where no demurrer can be pleaded, his work survives him. No good can be done but through some man's sorrow. It is enough for me to have laboured to a great end in books which have found favour from many indulgent readers. I look upon the public as a genial friend, in whose company one need never weary; and having worked, according to my most inadequate ability, to make some things better than they are, I can listen to the outcry of those whose illicit gains stand in jeopardy, without being much disturbed by it. 'It is an ill bird,' they say, 'who fouls his own nest.' True. But what should be said of the bird that seeks to cleanse it?

Unhappily, no evil can be attacked without saying some hard things of persons who gain by it.

Every man belonging to that class then seeks out the cap that fits him, puts it on his head triumphantly, as if he had made a discovery creditable to his discernment, and, though no personal affront was meant him, imprudently claims a right to be angry. Some people who go thus in search of grievances may be merely weak-minded folk, who are only doing wrong in an orthodox way, as their fathers did before them. They feel at once sore and ill-used, therefore, when their queer little trades are described in plain language. They believe that it is a proper and constitutional thing to wax fat in idleness, and to kick against all who interfere with their complacent enjoyment of other folks' goods. When I have been obliged to write home truths about them, I have always done so with reluctance; and have sincerely regretted that it was impossible to call public attention to much mischief in any other way.

After all is said and done, however, the pursuit of literature is scarcely satisfactory. When our best labours are over, we feel that so much might have been done which has been left undone, and that what has been done might have been done better. The opinions of a writer at the conclusion of his task are seldom precisely the same as when he began it, and the most thoughtful workman in revising his book will find some passages on which he would have bestowed more care, and others which he would, perhaps, have rejected altogether. I think, therefore, if I were to write these pages over again, I should treat some subjects with a sterner pen, and more emphatically denounce the follies and absurdities which I have touched here and there with too light a hand. Reader, farewell!

E. C. GRENVILLE MURRAY.

Paris, June 1, 1881.

# CONTENTS OF VOLUME I.

## FLIRTS.

| | | PAGE |
|---|---|---|
| I. | About Flirts in General | 9 |
| II. | The Flirt's Power | 20 |
| III. | The Flirt in the Season | 32 |
| IV. | The Flirt from Example and Precept | 45 |
| V. | The Flirt who has Plain Sisters | 59 |
| VI. | The Ecclesiastical Flirt | 69 |
| VII. | Regimental Flirts on Home Service | 83 |
| VIII. | The Regimental Flirt on Foreign Service | 93 |
| IX. | The Seaside Flirt | 103 |
| X. | The Tourist Flirt | 119 |
| XI. | Country-house and Town-house Flirts | 128 |
| XII. | The Sentimental Flirt | 135 |
| XIII. | The Studious Flirt | 142 |

## ON H.B.M.'s SERVICE.

| | | |
|---|---|---|
| I. | Introductory | 151 |
| II. | Ambassadors | 157 |
| III. | Envoys Extraordinary | 176 |
| IV. | Secretaries of Embassy | 183 |
| V. | Secretaries of Legation | 195 |
| VI. | Attachés | 203 |
| VII. | Consuls-General | 217 |
| VIII. | Consuls | 223 |
| IX. | Vice-Consuls | 229 |
| X. | Queen's Messengers | 235 |
| XI. | Interpreters | 244 |
| XII. | Ambassadresses | 248 |

## SEMI-DETACHED WIVES.

|  |  | PAGE |
|---|---|---|
| I. | INTRODUCTORY | 257 |
| II. | AUTHORESS AND ACTRESS | 261 |
| III. | SEPARATED BY MUTUAL CONSENT | 276 |
| IV. | CANDIDATES FOR A DECREE NISI | 287 |
| V. | A VERY VIRTUOUS SEMI-DETACHED WIFE | 303 |
| VI. | ULYSSES AND PENELOPE | 319 |

# FLIRTS.

## I.

### About Flirts in General.

OST persons possess some good qualities, know this, and wish others to know it. The process of making them known to one's own sex may be characterised under various names, while the endeavour to attract the opposite sex by them—and at the same time toying, as it were, with the passion of love—constitutes Flirtation.

One can obtain the appreciation of one's own sex by doing ordinary duties well; but to gain the good-will of the other sex, who may not be in a position to judge of our genuine merits, requires a manner more or less artificial. Flirtation is, therefore, a forced means of making oneself agreeable to a person of the other sex. In the greater or less transparency of the artifice lies the science of flirting which has infinite shades, from unblushing coquetry to the most delicate power of fascination. Society would be a dull thing without this science. If it were possible that women should cease for a short time to care what men thought about them, most of us, moralists or not, would be glad to see that short time ended.

Men and women flirt, but women more than men; and they also show it more. Women are less able than men to live without admiration, and have less other work in life than the labour of securing praise. At the same time they cannot so well keep their flirtations out of sight. A man travels, and is, in very few places, really intimately known; a woman is, in some few places at least, closely watched. None of a man's friends know precisely with how many women he flirts; a woman's friends keep an exact account of the number of her admirers. A man, to be called a Flirt, must flirt to the point of abandoning all other occupation; but a very little affability, squandered under the form of smiles, procures the title for a woman.

A girl is a Flirt who exchanges a coy glance with a middle-aged eligible bachelor who picks up a glove she has dropped; she is something worse than a Flirt—a minx—if she makes herself pleasant to another girl's betrothed. The iron rule of modesty, which men have imposed upon women as a protection against their wiles, leaves young women scarcely free to move or speak in the presence of the trousered sex without risk of being thought 'forward;' but women themselves are much sterner in their definition of forwardness than men. In feminine judgment every girl or pretty young woman is forward, and consequently a Flirt, who monopolises the attention of males in a social circle. This she can do by being too modest, as well as by being not modest enough; for her own sex will not account as modesty the grace which charms without attempting to do so. Men never speak so ill of the worst women as women do of the best among their sex who have the art of pleasing. There are men whom all other men join in praising; but there has scarcely lived a woman—wife, virgin, or saint—who has not had detractors amongst other women. Should there have been some few exceptions which prove this general rule, they will be found to have flourished in the ranks of the fearfully and unutterably ugly.

Every woman has flirted; but we are not concerned with the women whose innocent flirtations are but the gush of youthful spirits, or with those who owe the title of Flirt to the mere malignity of their own sex. The Flirts of whom we propose to treat are those who flirt of *malice prepense*. In these flirting is the art of sexual tantalisation.

It may also be termed, less philosophically, the art of playing with fire and getting scorched, more or less often. All Flirts burn themselves, once at least. Some squeal when they but singe their finger-tips, and retire straightway from the game with their eyes full of tears. These are third-class Flirts, having no real heart in the play. The recollection of their first smart makes them redden and tingle till they become old women, when, perhaps, they smile, and wish the burn could come over again. It was a third-class Flirt who, on the strength of a short and sharp acquaintance with the ways of the other sex, invented such sayings as 'Man is perfidious.'

The second-class Flirts get frequently burned without ever quite inuring themselves to the pain. They resemble dullish boys who play at football because they must, but never surmount the fear of being shinned. Sometimes the second-class Flirt

## ABOUT FLIRTS IN GENERAL. 13

gives up playing, and learns to laugh at her burns; more often she goes on till she can play no longer, and wearily sums up her experience of the sport as 'all burns and no pleasures.'

But the first-class Flirt cares not a pin for scorches. She is the salamander who lives in the fire. Sparks fly round her and she revels in them; she is all over scars, and surveys them complacently as a soldier does his wounds. Flirt from the nursery, Flirt in her teens, Flirt in her prime, she continues flirting when she is an old woman, and

flirts on her deathbed with the doctor. If she could come to life for a moment in her coffin, she would flirt with the undertaker. Commend us to this class of Flirt for making the heads of men flame like the tops of lucifer-matches. She sets quiet households a-fire; everything turns to tinder on her passage, and when she is buried an odour of brimstone hovers over her tomb. Her old lovers would be afraid to lift up the grave-slab that covers her lest they should see little blue-forked flames leap out diabolically.

We are not sufficiently versed in etymology to say when the word 'Flirt' first came into use, and from what it is derived. It seems to have dethroned the French *coquette*, which appears frequently in the writings of eighteenth-century authors; but coquette, which is described by some as a polite variant of *coquine*, and by others as the mere feminine of *coquet*, which, though it now means 'natty,' originally had the same signification as our English coxcombish, or *cock's*-comb. The word coquette is not much more than two centuries old. How were Flirts and coquettes called before that? The inconstancy of women is no new thing, alas; and though not catalogued in Scripture among the ills to which human flesh is heir, it drew many a dolorous ode from the earliest writers of Greece and Rome. Anacreon made epigrams on the subject; and Horace, in his plaintive lines to Barine, the 'terror of Roman mothers,' tells her that he could not believe her perfidious oath under any circumstances.

Matters had certainly not improved in the chivalrous ages, when knights spent half their time in fighting for their mistresses, and the other half in cursing their fickleness; and Francis I. is found scratching upon a window-pane, still to be seen in the Château de Blois,

> 'Souvent femme varie,
> Bien fol qui s'y fie.'

Shakespeare, who wrote under the reign of a Flirt, had plenty to say in disparagement of women, and drew many Flirts without giving them that name. Portia and Beatrice were both pretty fair triflers, and so was Rosalind, of whom her lover warbled:

> 'As the cat seeks after kind,
> So will lovely Rosalind.'

But a good apology for flirting is put into Othello's mouth when he says, in defence of Desdemona, that it is no reproach to a woman if she lays herself out to be pleasing. He subsequently departed from this view, when he smothered his wife; but this little piece of hastiness did not alter the soundness of his previous conclusions.

The truth is, that Shakespeare lived in an age when centuries of knight-errantry, joustings, floral games, courts of love, and what not, had taught women to think a vast deal of themselves. They flirted more than now, perhaps, only men had learned to bear it better. A poor wretch who had been fighting three years for his lady-love in the Holy Land returned to claim her after this probation: but their meeting befell on a day when it was pouring cats and dogs; whence it arose that the knight, as he threw himself at his mistress's feet with both knees in a puddle, besought her to get under shelter, and cast his mantle over her shoulders. The lady, instead of being touched by this care for her health, was indignant. 'What!' she exclaimed. 'If you have eyes to perceive that it rains at such a moment as this, you cannot love me!' And she condemned him, for his breach of gallantry, to remain silent for a whole year, if he would win her. That sort of thing would not do nowadays. It belonged to an epoch when women doled out their smiles economically, and thought a man well indemnified for wounds or chronic rheumatism by leave to kiss their finger-tips. A disgusted Scot, who seems to have been ahead of his age, wrote, in Jamie VI.'s time,

> ' O, the lasses o' the Cannongate,
> They are so wondrous nice ;

> They wulna gi'e a single kiss
> But for a double price.
>     Gar hang 'em! gar hang 'em!
>     Each upon a tree,
>     For I'll get as gude outside the gate
>     For a baubee!'

Did he get a good kiss for a baubee? We doubt it. He may have stolen the kiss and paid the baubee afterwards, as conscience-money; but the canny fellow's having appraised the lowest marketable value of a kiss at a halfpenny—worth a shilling of our money—goes far to show that this agreeable salutation was not held cheap. However, our Scotsman deserves to be noted as a social reformer, who protested against the airs which women were giving themselves. He said, 'Gar hang 'em!' as the Edinburgh mobs used to hang bakers in those days, when they sold their loaves too dear; and he advocated the cheapening of the relations between sexes, which is a boon not to be lost sight of among the other debts we owe to the Land o' Cakes.

A hundred years later a French courtier, visiting Scotland, was enabled to chronicle that an admirable feature in North British maidens was the fondness they showed for embracing strangers on both cheeks. There has since been a slight reaction in these matters; but never mind—every Scotch lassie now subscribes to the doctrine:

'Gin a body
Kiss a body
Need a body cry?'

It was the Puritans who, in England, first reminded women that they were made to suckle fools and chronicle small-beer. Drab gowns and a modest demeanour were the things they enjoined, and women have testified their appreciation of this reform by their unwavering retrospective allegiance to the Cavalier party ever since. Charles II. did but restore the reign of women for a brief space; and soon the Georgian era was to come, with its days of hard drinking, which turned men into sots, unfit to be flirted with. When gallants rolled under the table after dinner, of what power were soft glances and witching smiles? The bottle is woman's worst rival: she knows it; and the only wonder is that, in the fierce tussle for supremacy which now ensued between Drink and Woman, the receptacle for liquor should have been able to hold its own for more than a hundred years.

There never was such a graceless, loveless, flirtless period as the last century. Men treated women like tavern-wenches, and, having wooed them between two hiccoughs, eloped with them on the spur of a tipsy impulse. There were Mayfair marriages, Fleet marriages, and marriages at Gretna Green. The hot blood of the day, whiskified and lustful, was too impatient to brook a long courtship or the delay of banns or license. The Duke of Hamilton married one of the Misses Gunning with a bed-curtain ring; and abductions of heiresses by penniless rakes were so frequent that Parliament had to legislate on the matter. In that period of rowdy boozings, prize-fights, cock-fights, punch-clubs, and duels, society staggered, and its morals smelt of the bagnio. It was deemed a compliment to a woman to make her the

toast of a drunken orgy; and as many women passed over to the enemy, which they had fruitlessly combated, and began to drink as hard as the men, powder and patches came into fashion to hide flushed cheeks and swollen eyelids.

Pah! it reeks with a foul whiff, that corrupt eighteenth century; and nothing less than the five-and-twenty years' war which ushered in the nineteenth was needed to make its men sober and its women coy once more. In the life of camps the love for women burns with a purer light; and the brave are ever gentle, courteous, and timid towards the weak. Then poets arose amid the clash of our arms; and after Waterloo, Scott, Byron, Moore, and the Lakeists drew English thoughts towards chivalrous romance and pastoral idyl. The accession of a girl-Queen did the rest; and gradually, as the Sovereign's influence, as wife and mother, pervaded the Court, and spread thence over the people, woman's ascendency swelled to the full flood again, till it eventually overflowed, and feminised the whole surface of society.

We nowadays heap all our luxury on our women. Men have renounced the gold-laced coats, ruffles, and jewelry of their forefathers; but they cover their women with the costliest textures and with rivers of precious stones. Nothing is too plain or ugly for male attire, nothing too gaudy for woman's; and while the tailor's bill shrinks every year through the invention of rough colourless cloths impossible to wear out, the milliner's expands every season, because the ingenuity of *modistes* is for ever desiring tints so delicate that they can hardly bear the light, and trains so long that they are unfit for walking.

So much richness calls for display, and it is the ambition of the modern woman to show herself everywhere. She is no longer content with the empire of the drawing-room, ballroom, and theatre; she must reign in the open air; and sports have been invented—croquet, skating, and lawn tennis — in which she can mix with men and dwarf them. Balls have been multiplied for her sake, till there is not a householder with ten square feet of parlour but bids his friends once or

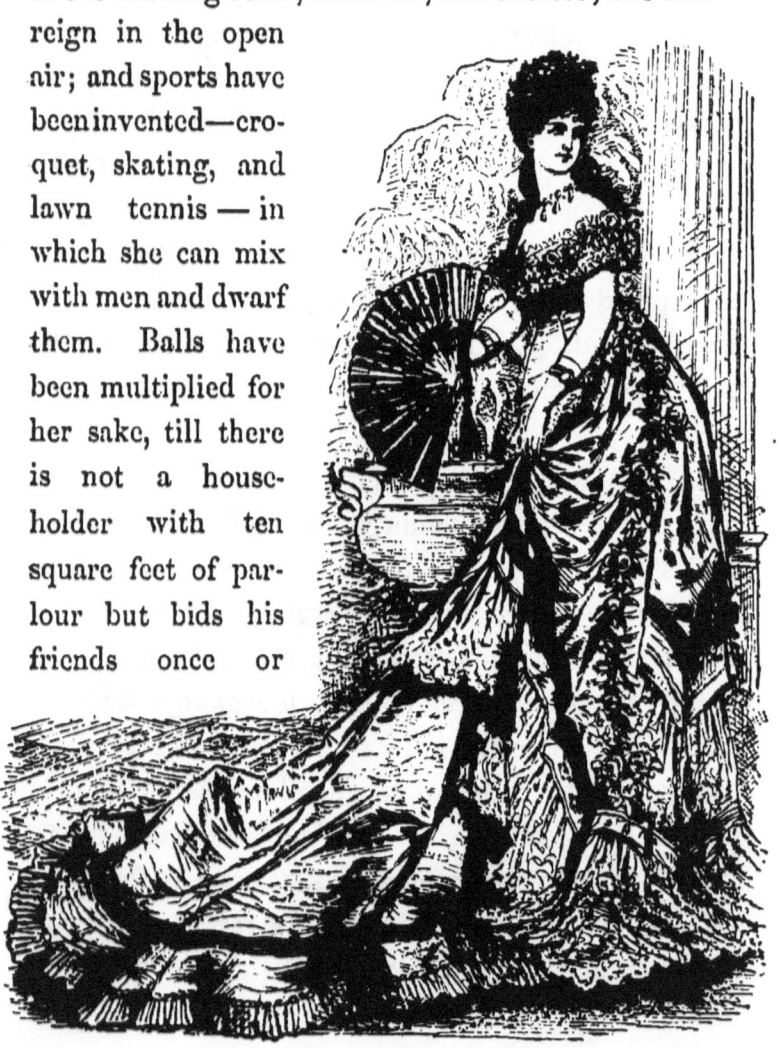

twice a year to a carpet dance; picnics have become the rage; water-parties and walking-tours exhibit woman's taste in fancy costumes, and her powers of hand and foot, for she does not disdain to pull an oar, and will back herself for a 'discretion' to walk long distances. She has invaded the hunting-field and shooting-covert; she has climbed on to the box-seat of four-in-hands; and reforming our

religion according to her own views of the æsthetic, she has given us Ritualism. The club remained, until lately, as a last refuge to man; but mixed clubs like the

Orleans and the Lotos have already been started, and, before long, woman will have forced open the doors of other houses. This will be the crowning triumph at which she has been aiming for years, and when she has achieved it, man's subjection will be complete. Then we shall see floating over White's and the Marlborough the emblem of female supremacy—a cambric handkerchief scented with opoponax.

## II.

### The Flirt's Power.

The goal of woman is marriage, and flirting is to girls a means of reaching the goal; in the case of married women it is a pastime, a consolation, or a vengeance. Both the girl and the married Flirt proceed by the same methods, though the one faces the goal and the other turns her back to it. The career of the former may close at the altar in great honour, that of the latter is apt to end with a tumble into the Divorce Court; for the essence of flirting is, that it is a stolen pleasure and a speculation, whose future results cannot be foreseen.

Flirting is, anyhow, a pleasant thing; and, without looking so far as to see how it ends, one may acknowledge it as a source of the most gratifying emotions obtainable on this earth. What would society be without it?—from the modest girl whose unconscious arts encourage the bashful lover to be bold, down to the experienced coquette, who shoots with an unerring aim glances that are meant to leave a festering wound. Every woman who flirts stimulates

AN EIGHTEENTH-CENTURY COQUETTE.

for the moment the vanity of the man whom she tries to please. Flirting is flattery in action. It may be so delicate as to leave a balm on the wounds it inflicts; and since of all forms of vanity the ambition to charm the other sex is, in both men and women, that which is first born and last dies, and which moreover rages strongest whilst it lives, there is no limit to the voluptuousness which may be caused by exciting it.

The imagination of the man who is flirted with expands into radiant visions; his blood flows in quicker pulses. Look at him when the eye of the coquette falls upon him deep and quiet, or light and playful, or with an electric flash. However worn and prosy he may be, his face beams, he throws out his chest, his voice is tuned into the softest inflections, or becomes uncontrollable from sudden emotion. So long as his charmer is within sight, he follows her with his gaze, dumbly soliciting a second glance, as a man holds out his glass to be refilled; and when she is gone, he glides into the most pleasing pensiveness. He is castle-building. No matter how often a man may have been mocked, the coaxing, caressing look of some new face, seen for the first time, will elevate him over present cares, and make him, it may be but for a brief instant, a poet. Eclogues and epics, fairer than have ever been printed, are composed daily in the hearts of commonplace men who could not rhyme two lines on paper; for every man is able to imagine himself the hero of a romance, and the woman who inspires that romance gifts him with the fancy to create a heroine.

Women would be too vain if they could realise the power of their seductions. It is lucky for men that they cannot. They themselves have no such impressionability as men, except in cases where their hearts or fortunes are deeply involved. A woman loves once in her life, and it is in the power of her lover to throw her, by a mere look, into shivering fits or silent ecstasies; she can also, on occasions, be made extremely wretched or happy by a man whom she does not love, but desires to marry. Save in these instances, however, she cares nothing for man's looks. A male Flirt may amuse, offend, or frighten her; but there will be no magic thrilling in her sensations, no giddy whirl of her mind, no castle-building. How coldly impervious a pure-minded woman can be to incendiary declarations was seen in poor Werther's case:

> 'Charlotte, when she saw his body
> Borne before her on a shutter,
> Like a well-conducted person,
> Went on cutting bread-and-butter.'

But supposing the situation had been reversed, and Charlotte, instead of a staid matron, had been a girl Flirt, setting her cap at Werther, a well-conducted married man, would Werther have remained insensible? Not likely. There is no use in denying that men cannot match women in callous propriety; for neither age, nor dignity, nor marriage-vows will steel them against the shafts of the Flirt.

A little saucy-eyed girl of seventeen will turn the

head of a prudent king, make a hoary statesman forget his intriguing business, and drive a pious bishop into terrible wrestling with the devil. It is this universal laxity in men's morals which arms women with their tremendous power—power of which, we repeat, few of them can guess the extent. But some of them do guess it in time, and make a wild use of their weapons of offence out of pure malice, and without a thought of deriving any advantage from their recklessness beyond the intimate satisfaction of having done mischief. Cruelty is no name for the heartless deliberation with which some of these pretty creatures will plunge a dagger into the heart which they have first set fluttering to assure themselves of its being alive.

Say, for instance, that a young man at the opera, standing up in the stalls between the acts to reconnoitre the boxes, lets his glance fall upon a woman of surpassing beauty. Their eyes meet, and she does not turn hers away, but examines the man a moment, smiles vaguely, and then goes on talking with her box-companion. But in another moment she has looked again at the man, and this time, when their eyes meet, a tinge of modest confusion overspreads her cheeks; she hesitates, then throws a wistful glance, which says, as plainly as possible, 'I wish we knew each other. I feel drawn towards you.'

One such glance suffices to set the man's heart

THE FLIRT AT THE OPERA.

"She sweeps by with the coldest of unconscious stares."

and head a-flame, and at the close of the performance behold him on the grand staircase waiting to see his charmer come out. But she is a practised Flirt, who has only amused herself by trying the killing-power of her eyes; just as a man, when going out to shoot, may prove his double-barrel by knocking a miserable sparrow off a branch, so, with the coldest of unconscious stares, she sweeps by, leaving the presumptuous wight dumbfoundered. He slinks off with a lagging step, out of conceit with himself, red to his ear-tips, and full of bile. It may be years before he recovers from this humiliation; and forget it he never will, if he lives to a hundred. There are some men who have carried the deep scar of one false glance all through their lives.

## III.

### The Flirt in the Season.

We prefer the Flirt with a purpose, who does not waste her powder upon sparrows, but finds a suitable object for every eye-shot. As we have said, there are innocent Flirts and guilty ones, and both can be seen during the London season flourishing in great numbers in all the resorts of festivity. The innocent Flirt, who comes out under a chaperon to hunt for a husband, begins operations bashfully. She is taken to be presented at one of the Drawing-rooms; and if it be a novel delight it is also a trying one to find herself driving down St. James's-street with bare shoulders in broad daylight. She sports a train three yards long, and a pearl necklace. On descending from their carriage in the palace-yard, she and her chaperon are surrounded by young men in showy uniforms, military, naval, and diplomatic, who bustle to offer their arms and murmur compliments. She is introduced to a youth in blue swallowtail and kerseymere breeches—an *attaché* home on leave— who begs to act as escort, and pilot her through the

THE FLIRT PRESENTED AT COURT.

crowded rooms, whilst a handsome young giant in the scarlet-and-gold of the dragoons does the same duty for the chaperon.

The press is so great and the scene so imposing that the bashful girl is glad to accept the arm of the sucking-diplomatist, who whispers to her the names of all the great people whom they jostle. Here a past premier with his star and garter; there a duchess and her daughter; there an archbishop and his wife; droves of admirals pushing nieces before them; and troops of generals doing their best for flocks of damsels who were the belles of garrison-towns. What a sight for a girl who has but just left the schoolroom, and who, not a year before, received her last whipping from a martinet governess!

The ceremony of curtsying to the Sovereign or the Princess cheek-by-jowl with the greatest personages in the land endows a girl with an assurance which never forsakes her afterwards. She perceives that the great are not so very formidable after all, and that good looks can hold their own even at Court. From the circle of princes and ministers grouped around the Throne, more than one admiring glance falls on her; and the Royal page who gathers up her train and chucks it over her arm as she retires from Royalty's presence does this more civilly than to titled dowagers with diamonds in their hair. Trust a girl, even a country-bred one, for noticing how many other girls, prettier than herself, there may be at one of these Drawing-rooms. The polite *attaché*, who joins her again after she has issued from the throne-room, mutters something nice about the grace with which she bears herself. He thinks her dress lovely, its train unique; and so forth.

The girl smiles; she only believes half those compliments (for she has had a first experience of flattery from country cousins at home), and yet she notices that guardsmen make way respectfully to let her pass; that grizzled veterans, whose breasts are covered with medals, nudge each other at her approach; and that sundry old ladies, with mortally plain daughters, eye her with that stony stare which, when it is levelled by woman at woman, is as good as purest incense. So, although her Majesty provides not so much as a cup of tea for the refreshment of her loyal subjects, who tire themselves in standing for hours in her saloons and other hours on the staircase waiting for their carriages, our incipient Flirt does not mind the fatigue. Her hair has got rumpled; her dress, disarranged in the crush, has lost half a yard of trimming; and one of her satin shoes is slipping off; but the *attaché* sticks close to her saying pleasant things, and the dragoon behind adds his word of testimony to the effect which her charms have produced. So this is to her a day of nectar-drinking. She has been presented at Court; she has had a success; and for that moment at least the world seems to be lying at her feet like a ball.

In a few days more she is in the very midst of the eddy of fashionable life. She returns from balls at

six in the morning, and does not leave her bed till midday. She has no sooner breakfasted than she must put on her habit for a ride in Rotten Row, where she wondrously soon gets to know the faces of the *habitués*, many of whom bow to her, whilst others wheel their nags round and canter by her side, asking her to promise them waltzes for the next dance at Lady A.'s or the Duchess of B.'s. At two she is

home again and dressing for an afternoon outing. One day there is a flower-show at the Botanical Gardens; on another a fancy bazaar; on another

THE FLIRT IN ROTTEN ROW.

some pigeon-shooting at Hurlingham. On Sundays there is the Zoo, varied by an occasional drive to Richmond, or a dinner at the Trafalgar at Greenwich.

At all these places the Flirt finds opportunities for airing her attractions, and practising those wiles which a girl learns as quickly as a kitten learns to frisk. She is noted for a beauty; her chaperon commends her for a sweet temper, enlarges on her talent as a pianist, and hints at 'expectations.' Matrimonial candidates are not wanting, and it becomes the Flirt's care to select the fittest. If she be a clever girl, she does this without offending anybody, and keeps the whole squad of her suitors still expectant up to the last moment, when, having booked an eligible offer, she can safely relapse into the chaste reserve of brides-elect.

The talent which some maidens show in thus playing off rival admirers against one another is something to see. If the heart does not get foolishly caught in the snares of some 'Detrimental,' the mind remains free to work out the problem of how to secure wealth and social position without too much self-sacrifice. A girl who may not be intent on marrying for love is yet anxious that her husband shall be kind; and the secret of so many oddly-matched weddings between brides in their teens and grizzly men past middle age is, that a girl often discovers that she has more chance of being tenderly treated by an old man than by a young one. Anyhow, she watches very keenly to see if the wooers who flit around her show signs of temper, stinginess, or jealousy.

She would not have much chance of enlightening herself on these points if her flirtations were confined to the morning rides or afternoon recreations above mentioned; but Ascot and Goodwood, the Eton and Harrow Match at Lord's, the *parties fines* at the Orleans Club, and the cotillons at balls enable her to study men for hours at a time, and to take her mental notes as to character. A man may conceal his defects during an afternoon; but it is rare when he does not let something of them peep out in the course of a day's excitement about horse-racing, or during a long cotillon, when he is made to go through figures in which he is converted into a laughing-stock, and must show how he can stand banter.

During Ascot week, for instance, the chaperon possibly hires a lodge near the course, goes to witness the four days' racing, and gives little dinners every evening to pleasant acquaintances whom she has met in the Grand Stand. Some of these inveigle the Flirt into betting. It used to be the custom for girls to bet gloves (when they did bet); but this has grown tame, and a girl now wagers hard money, or 'discretions'—which mean jewelry or a private settlement of a long milliner's bill. However, a Flirt would do well to be careful about indulging in this form of dissipation, for men do not really like a betting-girl. Many a smart miss has thrown a good matrimonial chance away by unguardedly taking a bet which had

been offered to prove her. Again, 'discretions' are awkward things, for, if a girl loses, the gallant gamester is apt to demand a settlement in the shape of a kiss, and to snatch it in a quiet corner, if voluntary payment be refused.

The Ascot week, however, is sure to bring instructive lessons. It is then that the Flirt sees how ill the sportive young baronet bears his losses on the turf, while the middle-aged merchant, who has, perhaps, lost three times as much, remains as serene as ever. The one stands revealed as a cantankerous cub; the other as a man of nerve and good taste. Race succeeds race, and the differences become more accentuated. In the evening, at dinner, the baronet is absent-minded and sour, talks of the villany of bookmakers, and swears that his favourite was 'roped;' the merchant overflows with anecdote, and proves that his appetite has not been impaired a jot.

The next day, at luncheon, on the top of a drag which has been tooled down from London by some noble member of the Four-in-hand Club, the young baronet drinks too much champagne, and his hand trembles as he holds up his field-glass to watch the start in a race on which he has risked a pot of money; the elderly merchant meanwhile devotes himself to the Flirt, and shows by his light chatting that he has an eye for something beyond the pecuniary aspects of a race. He points out the beauties of the course, the multicoloured line of jockeys breaking up for a preliminary canter, the picturesque effect of the mass of carriages thronging near the stand. Nor does he forget to make an appointment to meet his fair companion again at Goodwood, nor to mutter a few words about the attractions of his own country estate, which he

has just begun to plant with trees. There is no flattery like that of paying assiduous attention to a woman in despite of surrounding excitements; and at this game elderly men much excel young ones.

But the young ones come to the front again in ballrooms, and especially in cotillons. Of late years it has become the fashion to give calico-balls for the encouragement of native industry; so our Flirt is sure to appear once or more in the course of the season at one of these charitable hops, tricked out in some cheap stuff at fivepence a yard. A white-calico dress looped with bunches of scarlet tape, a red rose in her hair, and another at her girdle—this is her costume, and she contrives to create as much effect in it as if it had come from Worth's, in Paris. Your true Flirt always likes dancing, and seems never to tire. Her card is filled up within a few minutes of her entry into the ballroom, with the exception of the one or two dances which she reserves *in petto* for favourites; and she gaily trips through every valse and quadrille.

Middle-aged admirers are fain to play the wall-flower, and look on glumly during these untiring performances, which indicate a strength of muscle and a dashing disposition of mind not to be competed with by any man who has reached his fortieth year. The most prudent fogeys do not attempt to join in the dancing, sensibly recognising that those who take part in cotillons are apt to make exhibitions of themselves. A portly quadragenarian trotting over a polished floor with a grotesque pasteboard head on

his shoulders, or a bunch of canvas carrots in his mouth (for the humours of these cotillon figures are various), has often forced a Flirt to stuff her handkerchief between her lips. However, there is a cotillon figure where the ladies invite the gentlemen to dance; and here the Flirt may soothe an elderly lover's feelings by preferring him before younger men; or, again, she may gladden him by selecting his youngest and best-looking rival as the butt for all her malice, forcing him to sport the ass's head or the carrots, to gallop round the room on all-fours, and so forth. This can be done with the greater safety, as a young man is never displeased at being made to cut antics in cotillons.

## IV.

### The Flirt from Example and Precept.

Fanny is the Flirt-daughter of a Flirt-mother, who never had a chance of becoming anything else but a thorn to the other sex. Her parents were separated by mutual consent when she was about six years old, and she was taken to live with the one whom she knew and liked the least. But her mother was a beautiful creature, who won her admiration before securing her love: she was always so brightly dressed, so gay (when not out of temper), and she received such a number of well-dressed men in her drawing-rooms! Few ladies came; and little Fanny grew up to prefer gentlemen, because they took her on their knees and gave her bonbons.

Her mother's fits of temper were like rapid alternatives of cloud or sunshine. If things went wrong—if there were creditors or such-like annoyances—Fanny got slapped for nothing, and would run howling down to the kitchen to take comfort of the maid, a middle-aged sharp-eyed Frenchwoman, who was paid with mamma's cast-off dresses, and with vails from the visitors.

Fanny received no education to speak of; for her mother, who wanted her to play Propriety in the drawing-room when she received visitors, or in the carriage when she drove in the Park, could not think of sending her to school. Sometimes a governess came to give her lessons; but governesses and mamma had a trick of quarrelling, chiefly about Fanny's backwardness and the impossibility of making her learn anything so long as her mother encouraged her in idleness and saucy ways. When mamma was in a good-humour she would have Fanny brought into her dressing-room, and spent hours in covering her with finery, combing her hair, and washing her hands in milk of almonds to make them white. She said that the wild little mite had the same blue eyes as herself; and she took pleasure in hearing gentlemen say that she would grow up as pretty as a fairy.

The time came, however, when Fanny was called up less and less often into the presence of visitors.

This was when she had reached her tenth year, and began to look too much of a hoyden for a mother who wished to appear perennially twenty-five. As a consequence, she took to living a great deal with the servants in the kitchen. They employed her to fetch and carry, and opened her small mind wonderfully with their tattle. She could hardly read large print, but was aware that the potman courted Sue the housemaid, and that when a certain policeman looked over the area-railings, softly whistling, he was after Meg the cook. Then she learned what duns meant, and saw many of them parleying with Jack the page-boy, a precocious imp, who treated her on terms of easy familiarity, and got her to steal pomatum and scented soaps for him out of her mother's dressing-room. By and by this lad informed her that 'missus' was going to 'old Gooseberry,' which he explained to mean 'blue smash,' or anything else that signified bankruptcy.

The servants did not receive their wages regularly, and set meals were no longer the rule in the dining-room. Fanny therefore ate with the servants, while her mother took breakfast in bed and generally dined out. Sometimes mamma would vanish for six weeks together to Paris or the seaside, and on her return rate Fanny sharply for looking such a slut. The truth is Fanny enjoyed her mother's absences; for they allowed her to go gadding about with the servants, who took her to Rosherville, and wound up the

THE FLIRT IN HER TEENS.

"The curate's male progeny fight with their fists for the honour of dancing attendance on her."

excursion with a happy evening at some music-hall, where she and the precocious page drank negus out of the same tumbler. This blissful life was abruptly interrupted when Fanny was fourteen. An execution was put into the house. 'Fanny's mother contrived to secrete her jewels, and went off to the Continent with them; and Fanny herself was sent to reside with a distant connection, a curate in Yorkshire.

It was three years before the mother and daughter met again, and by that time Fanny had learned to read, write, gabble French, and strum three tunes on the piano. The curate's wife imparted to her such knowledge as she possessed; the curate teased her with moral lectures; but on the whole she rather enjoyed her life at the parsonage, where she had plenty of playfellows, and was held in some respect by reason of her London experiences. She became a romp, and had the pleasure of seeing the curate's male progeny fight with their fists for the honour of dancing attendance on her. She was just sixteen when Tom, the eldest boy, who was fourteen and a half, proposed they should elope together, and set up house with eleven and sixpence he had saved out of his pocket-money. She flew at rather higher game in accepting the advances of a country-town baker's heir, who paid his court by presenting her with small fruit-pies, which he made surreptitiously with his father's flour. This flirtation was in a fair way towards driving the young baker to commit suicide in one of his own ovens, when Fanny was called away

from the parsonage to join her mother, who had returned to London, and expressed her intention of bringing her daughter 'out.'

Fanny was rather sorry to leave the parsonage for the purpose of resuming what she remembered as a life of discomfort; but she found her mother much changed. By some arrangement with Fanny's father all debts had been paid, and the separated wife was to enjoy a handsome allowance payable monthly, but contingent on no further debts being contracted. Later on the daughter discovered that this arrangement had been effected by parentally defrauding her of some property to which she was entitled under her mother's marriage settlement. Anyhow, the maintenance allowed was sufficient to keep mother and child in decent state. They had a brougham, a footman, a well-furnished house in the West-end, and a margin to buy an occasional opera-box with. Fanny learned that she was to become her mother's bosom friend and companion, and do her best to catch a husband who should provide them both with a sumptuous establishment.

Fanny was exceedingly pretty, and her queer bringing-up had rendered her knowing as a young cat. She was not slow to discern that her respected mother was selfishness in petticoats, and only set store by her as a marketable commodity; nevertheless, she took a semi-contemptuous liking for the faded, light-headed, garrulous lady, who initiated her into the arts by which men may be cozened. Not that such arts really need teaching like an abstruse science, for women pick them up intuitively; but young Flirts

can always learn something from older ones, especially when these older ones know the fortune and parentage of every man in society.

Fanny went to balls, and her mother told her afterwards the exact worldly position of every partner with whom she had danced. She bade her beware of 2000*l.* a year, which is but gilded misery; 5000*l.* with landed property, said she, was too often comparative pauperism, for the land ate up most of the income; 10,000*l.* a year derivable from a bank or manufactory, and with an M.P.ship annexed, would do as a *pis-aller;* but it would be foolishness not to pitch one's ambition on the best things at once, and go in straight for a coronet and 50,000*l.* per annum. Such prizes, she told her, frequently fall to the lot of girls who have nothing but their good looks to bring their husbands. Fanny, who began to think no small champagne of herself on finding her beauty attract general notice, laid the maternal maxims to heart, and trifled with a great number of suitors whom most other girls in her position would have been glad to catch. She did not flout them, but behaved worse— leading each one on separately to hope and hope till, finding a better, she dropped him as unceremoniously as a spoilt flower.

During her first season she was all the rage. Afterwards at Spa, and during a round of visits in country houses, she kept eligible men round her in shoals; but she was too giddy to see that such chances as she then had would never come again, and she became noted for an incorrigible Flirt before the novelty of dancing upon men's hearts and vanities had in any way begun to pall upon her. During her second season she was less in vogue than the first; but setting it down for a dull season, she adjourned her hopes without losing any of her illusions. At her third season, however, her eyes opened somewhat,

for she who had flirted with everybody began to be flirted with in her turn by men who made fun of her.

This is always a sign of decadency. Fanny's mother grew cross, and accused her of not knowing how to play her cards; the girl retorted with vehement recriminations, and there were some fine screaming scenes between the attached couple. On the whole, Fanny's mother did wrong to initiate quarrels, for she had everything to lose by wounding the girl's pride. Fanny took a brooding resolution, that when she married it should be for herself alone, and that she would never allow her mother to set foot in her house.

She insensibly lapsed into the second manner of Flirts, which is one of great softness. She saw that several men whom she had rejected had married, and were both prosperous and happy—which made her jealous and cautious, but not more easy to please; for looking at her marriage from a purely personal point of view, she was now unconsciously more fastidious than when she regarded it as a speculation in which her mother was to have a half share. On the other hand, men, knowing her to be a Flirt, were not duped by her softened manner; and many held aloof who would have urged their suits if they could have believed she would have treated them *au sérieux*.

She was still so pretty as to seem a most desirable acquisition to men who count beauty for much in the choice of a wife; and she had a small tender spot in her heart—just enough to keep her romantic after many deceptions. So it befell that one bright day she began to take a serious interest in one of her love-affairs with a young gentleman of property.

The wooer had good looks and good temper on his side; and she really liked him—so much so that her cheeks flamed and her pulses throbbed on several occasions when she thought a proposal was impending. But he heard of her reputation, turned shy, and suddenly jilted her—by which blow she was nearly driven out of her senses. For several days it seemed to her as if life had lost all its savour—all its prospects; then she rallied, and, becoming reckless from her humiliation, threw herself at the head of the first man who offered himself. This person chanced to be a middle-aged archæologist, who was as much embarrassed as flattered by the hazard which put him in possession of a young, brilliant, and very expensive wife, much too skittish for him to manage.

His archæological studies were not benefited in consequence. Flirts like Fanny do not make good wives. The girl had married more to spite her mother than to please herself; and once she had exhausted the pleasure of seeing her parent gnash her teeth, she found out that she had mated herself to a man by no means congenial to her tastes. The archæologist had married in order to have a home; Fanny wanted to enjoy her privileges as a matron by gadding about to amusements too costly for her husband's purse. In their early days of connubial bliss, when free from the rheumatic attacks to which a

## THE FLIRT FROM EXAMPLE AND PRECEPT.

misplaced ardour on the subject of lake dwellings had rendered him liable, her husband used to escort her on these occasions; but he soon grew tired of his *rôle*. A demand for extra pin-money produced a coolness between the couple; the first milliner's bill, about a yard in length, occasioned a decided breach. Fanny's mother did not help to mend matters, for, being called in as an ally by her reconciled and repentant daughter, she went to work as mothers-in-law not unfrequently do, and entered her protest against the marital theories of economy. Then daily bickerings arose, stinging speeches and mutual recriminations; all of which ended at last by the archæologist making a cheerful surrender of half his income for the sake of seeing his wife and her mother leave his house together.

Thereupon the husbandless pair of Flirts resumed their old life in company. It was not a joyous life. For the young wife especially it became a weary round of dissipations, which, being now aimless, was bereft of all zest. She could not marry again whilst her husband was alive, and the continuance of her alimony depended on her not breaking any of the commandments that concern marriage. On the whole, Fanny learned, rather too late, that flirting is a wind which seldom blows light craft on a prosperous voyage.

## V.

### THE FLIRT WHO HAS PLAIN SISTERS.

In the catalogue of Flirts this variety has many representatives. England is a country of large families; all the girls in a family cannot be pretty, and it will often happen that amongst half a dozen sisters, one only has any pretensions to comeliness. This one is called 'the Beauty,' and she becomes in a household what the 'favourite' is in a racing-stable. All the family hopes are centred upon her, and she is expected to win good matrimonial stakes for herself that she may provide well for her sisters afterwards.

Her sisters do not much like her as a rule—how should they? She eclipses them whenever they appear together: she is a butterfly, and they so many gray moths. Nevertheless Beauty is not treated in the Cinderella fashion, for that is a style which has grown antiquated. Nowadays Cinderella's ugly sisters would have calculated the advantages of possessing a relative who could bring them to great honour, and comfort them on every side.

Besides, Beauty often has a mother who keeps the

ugly sisters in subjection. Appraising with maternal shrewdness the perfections of the one child who is

the living image of what she herself was, or thinks herself to have been, the judicious parent gives out that Beauty is delicate, and requires special petting—

that she is also a very sensitive child, and must not be teased. With more or less good grace, the sisters submit to see Beauty lie in bed longer than they, wear prettier dresses, and drink a glass of port-wine every day at luncheon. Jealousy goads them to snub the favoured one now and then with tart speeches, or to pinch her slyly in corners and plead provocation—which does not save them from correction at the maternal tongue or hands.

It is more pleasing to reflect that in frequent cases the ugly sisters join quite as cordially as their mother in the recognition of Beauty's queenship. If they be a well-taught good-natured family in straitened circumstances—say, the daughters of a country clergyman—it becomes evident to them that they cannot all go up to London to enjoy themselves at balls and flower-shows; so they get to feel a sort of pride in the sister who is to wear the family colours, and, whilst enjoying her winsome face, wish it luck for their own sakes. These are beauties who have been passionately loved and admired by their ill-favoured kin.

In any case, Beauty is sure to be spoiled by the family acknowledgment of her charms; and by the time she is consigned to the London aunt or godmother who has undertaken to bring her out, she has formed rather rosy anticipations of the triumphs that await her. Nobody has exactly told her that she has been sent to London to catch a husband; but she

understands what hopes have been placed upon her, and feels that she is not intended to return home unengaged. However, her first parties in town cause her a sharp disappointment. She passes unnoticed among the crowd of other beauties; she is jostled on staircases; her chaperon has actually to finesse in order to find her partners; and these, far from being overwhelmed by her charms, treat her with remarkable composure, and talk a drawling *persiflage* which she does not understand.

All this is very different from what Beauty had

expected, on the faith of a society experience derived from three-volume novels. She had pictured well-dressed men of title and fortune thronging round her in circles five deep; and a particular one, dark, very tall, calm, muscular, sardonic towards men and gentle as a lamb towards herself, who should do violent things in her honour, and eventually win her hand by cowing all his rivals like a very lion-tamer. A country Flirt has always to unlearn a great deal when she comes up to town; and the intermediary period between the discarding of old ideas and the acquisition of new puts her in much the same shivering plight as moulting birds, when their worn feathers have gone and the fresh brilliant plumage is growing. This morally denuded plight is also one full of peril.

Beauty may let herself be caught unawares by a sapient fowler, whose snares were too cunning to be suspected. Feeling that even the smooth places of society are strange to her tread, how can she guess its pitfalls? The jargon of ballrooms; the indifference which everybody seems to express towards everything; the competition with other beauties whom she sees to be prettier, sprightlier, gayer than herself; and, above all, the bewildering whirl of new faces: these things abash her. It appears to her as though she never met the same persons twice. Every day brings fresh introductions; so that a partner whom she chances to encounter at three different houses in the course of a fortnight gladdens her like an old friend. This partner is a fowler, and in Beauty's artless welcome of him lies his chance.

But the chaperon is watchful. Beauty is warned that the partner is a Detrimental, and so learns her first lesson of the dangers of town. If she escapes the danger by treating Detrimental guardedly on the fourth occasion of their meeting, she is in a manner seasoned, and walks thenceforth with a securer foot.

Then comes her bright time, when she discovers that the position of a belle during the London season is not quite what she had dreamed. It is nevertheless a pleasant position after all. Her aunt need take no trouble now to find partners for her. The circle of her acquaintance gradually expands, till it includes nearly a couple of hundred unmarried men, whose names she cannot remember, and of whom she knows nothing more than what they have told her about themselves between the figures in a quadrille or during the panting halts of a waltz. Not having memory enough to recollect all these physiognomies, she is often surprised when a man whom she had taken for a stranger comes up and asks her to dance, on the strength of an introduction at a previous ball.

Some partners—officers, government clerks, or young barristers—have the polite effrontery to tell her, in so many words, that she is an uncommonly pretty girl. The first time she turns scarlet; but perceiving her complimenter whisper, a few minutes afterwards, in the ear of another pretty girl, who merely giggles, she takes such free-and-easy banter for what it is worth, and learns to be surprised at nothing.

Meanwhile, from out of the two hundred men who have been presented to her, a dozen or so, who habitually move within her aunt's 'set,' turn up more often than others; and among these, again, some half dozen are pronounced by her aunt to be 'very nice,' which, in her phraseology, means 'eligible.' London lives much in sets; and Beauty has to cure herself of the delusion that her range of choice is unlimited. Towards the end of the season she gets somehow to see that she may really have the pick of three out of the eligible six, and that the result of three months' dancing, dressing, and sight-seeing is that she must choose at short notice whether she will marry a junior partner in an indigo firm, a solicitor of forty in rising practice, or a shy squire of thirty, who looks down at the carpet and traces patterns on it with the point of his boot while he is speaking to her.

Good-bye to visions of dashing earls with commissions in the guards, to tall dark muscular men with lamb-like manners, and to all the big prizes in the marriage lottery! The plain fact has to be faced—that Beauty's aunt cannot afford to take charge of her for a second season; and that the girl must make her selection and seal her fate before society 'goes out of town;' failing which she will have to return home and shift for herself as she can amongst those ugly sisters of hers.

It is really a very trying moment, and it seems to the girl as though events had rolled with such steam-like rapidity that the end of the season has come before she has had time to look about her. Nobody has won her heart, and it does not strike her that any of the three gentlemen above mentioned evinces the signs of a violent passion towards herself. Her aunt hints that the rising solicitor is an admirable man, so prudent, wise, and well-to-do; but Beauty prefers the shy squire, because he seems kind and manageable, which the solicitor does not. The lawyer soon perceives this, and, having no time to waste, retires from the contest in a huff, which so piques the aunt that she reads Beauty a sharp lesson upon giddiness; whereon Beauty, feeling miserable, vents her wretchedness by a fit of sulking towards the squire, who, taking fright, after one particularly depressing *tête-à-tête*, retires also.

These calamities leave only the indigo partner in the field; but Beauty cannot rally in time to snatch at this man without knowing anything of his character, as she says. He seems pert and perky; he talks of everything with disparagement; and Beauty does not think she could be happy with him, at least not till she has had time to study him a little more. So at a final garden-party she neglects to give him the necessary amount of encouragement; the next day he leaves a *p.p.c.* card; and the aunt informs Beauty, with a mixture of anger and pity, that the season is over now, and her chance at an end. 'I've done my best for you, my dear; but girls nowadays are not what they were in my time. *We* always knew when to be serious. *We* were aware that men can't be trifled with, for pretty faces are as plentiful as blackberries; and it is quite a mistake for a girl to suppose that if she flirts with a man, he can't go away and find just as good as herself anywhere.'

Beauty is surprised to hear that she has been flirting. It appears to her as though the swift round of society amusements had left her no leisure to do anything half so deliberate. She goes home disconsolate enough; and perhaps two years later, after having in the mean time eked out the weariest of existences with her ugly sisters, she marries a farmer or a curate. But to the end of her life the recollection of her one London season lingers in her mind as a phantasmagoria, a whirligig, a dervish dance, and she decides that she did not get fair play in being blamed for not having chosen a husband in the so rare intervals of thought that were left her between one pleasure and another. Country beauties cling a long time to the fallacy that husband-choosing is a matter for reflection, wherein they differ from their town sisters.

BEAUTY'S SINGLE LONDON SEASON.

"The aunt informs Beauty that the season is over and her chance at an end."

## VI.

### The Ecclesiastical Flirt.

The desire of bishops to promote their sons-in-law has long been notorious and praiseworthy. A bishop may educate his son and leave his promotion to others; for too many dignitaries of the bishop's own surname, holding his appointments, would cause a scandal; but a son-in-law bears a different family name, so his advancement is a much easier matter. For this reason the clerical candidates for the hand of a right reverend lord's daughter are always numerous and eager.

It does not follow that a bishop's daughter always cares to marry a clergyman. Bishops are of many sorts: the worldly-minded, the scholarly, the pious, and the ascetical. The two first categories generally take their families to town during the parliamentary session; the last two leave them in their dioceses and go to London alone, lodging *en garçon* under the hospitable roof of Lambeth Palace, where three sets of rooms are reserved in Lollards' Tower for prelates in their case. Now a girl whose episcopal father belongs to a noble family, and obtained his mitre solely owing to his connections, is rather disposed to wed a landowner or a soldier than a priest; again, the daughter of an ex-college don or public-school head-master has hankerings after a life different from that which she has led among cloisters or collegiate closes. Her father's promotion is sure to have elated her ambition a little. She thinks man is seen at his best in a scarlet coat. She wonders what a military messroom can be like. She has read in novels that officers are gallant cheerful fellows, who make their spouses lead merry lives; and all that she has seen of them herself— their startling clothes when out of uniform, their moustaches and eyeglasses, nay, the odour of the choice cigars they smoke—have a tantalising effect upon her senses. There were no cigars smoked in her father's household, and she had indeed learned to connect the use of tobacco with a precocious depravity of morals; for her right reverend parent, when he was head-master of Whippingham Grammar School, used to birch, with merciless severity, boys who were caught polluting themselves with smoke in secret corners.

The don-bishop's daughter, if she be pretty, seldom abandons herself to excessive devotion. Her father (whom much scholarship has converted at heart into a semi-pagan) rather discourages that kind of thing, as tending to trouble and social indignity. Whilst he was a schoolmaster he inculcated attendance at chapel as a duty; likewise the reading of pious books on Sundays, because they conduced to learning as well as edification. Religion and lessons were so inseparably connected in the girl's mind that the mere sight of a 'Paley' or 'Butler' recalled tedious Sunday tasks, while the reading of a collect in church stirred memories of bygone Sabbaths, when these pithy prayers had to be learned by rote and recited to a governess before breakfast under pain of bad marks.

A don's daughter (if pretty as above said) is seldom a lover of books, pedagogic ways, or academical or ecclesiastical architecture. A tender remembrance and liking for these things may come back to her in afterlife, when she has long lived apart from them; but while growing in her teens she can imagine nothing more dull than to vegetate all one's days in an atmosphere of ink and schoolroom stuffiness. She envies the boys or undergraduates when they go away for the vacations; and if she can get acquainted with some of them whom her parents occasionally invite to tea, she prefers the society of those who can talk with her about scenes having nothing to do with rectories or scholastic institutions. She looks down upon clergymen's sons; and herein takes after her parents, who show much more favour to the boys whose fathers own broad acres or prosperous banks.

The compensation which a don's daughter obtains for her otherwise tiring life is the having plenty of young male eyes to admire her. She gets her first schooling in vanity from marking how the fifth-form boys stare at her and nudge each other as she walks into chapel with her mother. If her beauty have shone forth very early, doubtless one of the young cubs, bolder than the rest, takes to ogling her, and finds an opportunity for sending her some anonymous doggerel. He also shows off his prowess for her in the cricket-field or on the river, getting bowled out by a full-pitch or catching crabs in the gallant attempt to overdo himself. These things may cause the don's daughter to smile, but they afford her early practice in flirting; so that by and by, when her father is promoted to the pomp of lawn-sleeves, she is ready to try her proficiency in the wider arena of fashionable life. Hazard, which plays many pranks, may not unlikely throw in her way the identical young gentleman who made such good use of his bat in her honour; and if he turn out to have property or prospects, and to be as pleasant and enterprising as in his days of puppyhood, missy may possibly close her career as

THE ECCLESIASTICAL FLIRT.

"The fifth-form boys stare at her and nudge each other as she walks into chapel with her mother."

a Flirt by taking him for better or worse. Pedagogue bishops often catch as sons-in-law adults whom they have whipped in youth, and would sometimes like to whip again.

Matters are different with the daughters of bishops of the pious or ascetic sort. By these are meant prelates of rigidly Low-Church views or highly developed Ritualists, but in both cases earnestly religious bishops, not pedagogues or men of the world. Such men have usually been rectors of large parishes, or preaching canons noted for controversy. Their zeal has spread to their families. Wife, sons, daughters, have all enrolled themselves under the banner of the Church Militant; and the daughters especially desire nothing better than to continue in ecclesiastical harness all their lives by being paired off with clergymen of congenial zeal, snugly beneficed.

Clerical fervour is so apt to impart primness to young ladies that the daughter of a religious bishop is generally a demure puss, of starched ways and great inner slyness. She wears her hair smoothed down in bands, affects black dresses with plain collars and cuffs, and descants gravely upon the sin of worldliness to her class at the Sunday-school. For all this she has a knowledge of the temptations of the flesh and the ways of the devil, such as is not to be matched by any individual amongst her father's

clergy; whilst on points of doctrine she could outargue a refractory archdeacon. Her mode of flirting consists in propounding to young clergymen questions to test their orthodoxy; and the compliments she best relishes are those implied in an unreserved surrender to the law, which she lays down with far greater promptitude and decision than the Court of Arches. If her proclivities be towards High Church, she adorns her album with photographs of Messrs. Mackonochie, Purchas, Bennett, and Tooth, and can recapitulate volubly, in tones of muffled indignation, all the counts upon which these just men were unjustly condemned at law. If she be of Evangelical bias, she deplores the relapses towards the errors of Rome, and cherishes a scheme for bringing Baptists, Shakers, Quakers, and Jumpers all within the Anglican communion.

To do this sort of ecclesiastical maiden justice, she seldom dallies long with the divine whom she makes up her mind to choose; and what is more, she is very prone to select a curate who has little else but the clothes in which he stands, superadded to the physical or moral qualities which have rendered him lovable. There is in this much calculation, mixed up with love and a modicum of Christian charity, for Miss Prim knows the advantage of becoming wife to a friendless divine, who has no power of himself to help himself. She is far too shining a light to be hidden under a marital bushel. She must be mistress not only in her new home—which is her incontestable right—but in her future husband's parish, which might not seem so much a matter of right if the said husband derived that parish from other hands than hers. Trust her for taking care that her bridegroom gets the fattest benefice in her father's gift at the

time of her engagement, with a promise of transfer to other and fatter ones as fast as they become vacant; and depend upon it, she feels no manner of scruple for the unstinted use which she makes of my lord's patronage on behalf of the consort whom she is pleased to regard as a 'chosen vessel.'

Unfortunately bishops are not lords temporal but lords temporary, and the good things which they can dispense when alive are not to be bequeathed at their deaths. Prelates' daughters have sometimes found out that this drawback operates very much to their eventual humiliation and misery. Clerical husbands who have been uxorially driven by wives who wielded their father's croziers, so to say, have been known to jib—nay, to kick out—when their right reverend fathers-in-law had been laid in the cathedral vaults, where no more loaves and fishes could be got out of them. But such cases are really so painful that one had better not pursue the matter further.

We come now to the Ecclesiastical Flirt, who is the daughter of a plain parson, never destined to attain episcopal honours. The position of girls whose fathers are clergymen in straitened circumstances has at all times been difficult, for the children of a gentleman aspire to marry persons of gentle rank, whereof the supply is not always equal to the demand in lonely parishes. Doubtless, when it comes to the hard pass of marrying a tradesman or remaining single, the country clergyman's daughter generally

decides not to bide a virgin; but years must have

ripened her face and judgment pretty considerably before she acknowledges that she is reduced to the stiff alternative; commonly her early prime is wasted in the waiting for the wooer of suitable fortune and station whom she imagines to be always coming, and who so seldom does come. Thus it is that the country parson's daughter flirts with every eligible man within reach.

She has the curate (it was she who first discovered that dear papa wanted some assistance); she has the parish doctor, whom she makes every excuse for consulting, not on her own behalf, for her plan is to be always counted as healthy, but on account of dear papa or of some pet parishioners; and again, the parish doctor's assistant, or his medical friend, the young Sawbones, fresh from Guy's, who comes and stays with him for a week. Then the squire's son takes lessons from the rector at uncertain intervals, and calls frequently with trout or hothouse flowers, for which the rector's daughter thanks him gushingly; and with so much ecstatic phrasing on her love for flowers that the young hobbledehoy ends by wishing he had let the flowers be.

It is upon the bachelor vicar of the neighbourhood that the rectory Flirt has all the while set her heart. She delicately hints he must feel very strange, all alone in that queer old house? Asks who helps him

in visiting the women? Who looks to the efficiency of the schoolmistress? Is he not afraid of getting into eccentric bachelor habits, like dear old Mr. A., who is never fully dressed till 2 P.M.; or that good Mr. B., who has not dined out for seven years, except on Easter Monday? If he should be ill, will he be sure and let her know? She can nurse; she nursed poor aunt Jane in her last illness.

The unmarried vicar listens to all this half-sheepishly, but he has to hear a good deal more. He is really a fish so well worth netting that his colleague's gushing child leaves him no peace. Her father, she says, is the last of the old yeomen; her great-grandfather was knighted; her mother is the daughter of a rural dean. She—the gushing child—wants occupation. She cleans the church, and decorates it at Christmas and Easter. She will decorate his if he likes. She always reads the *Parish Magazine*, the *Penny Post*, and the *Record* (or *Church Times*, as the case may be). Will he help her to keep up her French? Might she offer to teach him music? Mamma cannot go out much; will he take their house on his rounds? He will always find some one at home (a slight simper and twinkle in the eye give emphasis to the words 'some one'), and she will be so happy if he will come more often and take a quiet cup of tea!

Here the child becomes pensive, and strikes a pathetic vein. She has had some thoughts, says she, of becoming a 'sister.' Does her friend advise her to take that course? She feels so lonely sometimes, having no one to care for, and be understood by, that she thinks it would be a relief to her to don the nun's habit and spend her life in doing good. He must not talk of leaving the parish—what would the poor do without him? Of course he has enemies; every truly good man has; but some of whom he little dreams are taking his part in everything. She could not bear to think that if he went away she should never see him again.

There is something wondrous pitiful in these struggles which the smaller sort of Ecclesiastical Flirt has to make in the hunt after a husband and an establishment; and it is dismal to relate that so much finessing is mostly wasted. Bachelor vicars have a partiality for brides who can bring them a little money, and who, besides, entertain towards the clergy that soothing reverence which is not often felt by parsons' daughters who have lived among 'the cloth' all their lives. However, a man who marries a parson's daughter seldom makes a very bad bargain. These young ladies turn out better than their brothers are proverbially supposed to do, although it certainly is a fact that if a parson's daughter, through disappointment in legitimate flirting, branches off on the down-road to the pit of destruction, she mostly takes a clean header off the brink, and goes to the very bottom of that pit at one jump.

## Regimental Flirts on Home Service.

The 'garrison hack,' as she is more humorously than respectfully called, has been the heroine of a hundred novels; and she is a type true to every country that boasts an army—save Turkey, perhaps, where women are kept locked up.

The British army differs from others, however, in being largely officered with rich men, and so the daughters of its colonels and majors have finer opportunities than their sisters in other lands. In France, officers are so notoriously poor that a War-Office regulation obliges a lieutenant to sign a declation on his word of honour that the young lady whom he wishes to marry has a dower of at least 1000*l*. The dower for captains is 1600*l*., and so on; and yet it seems that numerous French officers marry on no more than the regulation dower, and contrive to rub along somehow not unpleasantly. In England, marriage is often a saving to an officer, inasmuch as it withdraws him from mess. If a linesman have 500*l*. a year of his own besides his pay he will generally find it cheaper to set up a house with a sensible little woman than to run up bills for expensive dinners, and squander his substance in cards, bets, and billiards. But needs must that a man should be in the infantry to find marriage a paying business; for the sensible little woman who weds a cavalry officer thinks herself bound to keep up a certain state, and she will ride because her husband does. Two chargers for

the captain, a hack for the little woman, a pony-carriage, grooms, and all the rest of it, mean 1500*l*. at once, putting things at the lowest figure; so if a hussar or dragoon cannot command that much, matrimony in his case is the preliminary to sending in his papers.

This being so, there is a marked difference between the cavalry and the infantry Flirt. The former stands several pegs above the latter, and is altogether a gayer, bolder, and faster strategist. She has to

manœuvre among richer men—some very rich—and she seldom pitches her ambition, to begin with, on anything lower than a landed estate and a town house. Her tone may be more or less loud—that depends on the regiment with which she is connected—but she knows that the cavalry never go in for cheapness or humdrum amusements, and she mostly forces her own tastes somewhat in order to keep pace with the jolly companions from whose midst she hopes a husband will some day slip out.

Here it is worth remarking that girls seldom in their hearts enjoy fastness. That proverb about every woman being at heart a rake may be more or less true, but it means in any case that women like a little quiet rakiness indoors—not the boisterous recreations of the other sex. A girl often schools herself to an apparent passion for hard riding, stout, underdone meats, furious waltzing, lawn-tennis, and even shooting pheasants; but the pangless way in which she surrenders these pastimes after marriage proves how little she inwardly cared for them. Civilisation cannot obliterate nature nor wholly transform woman, who is a stay-at-home bird, into a scourer of hedgerows and fields. But girls take, by the instinct of vanity and of sexual attraction, to the occupations which are likely to bring them most into contact with men; and if they think that fastness pleases the males who surround them, they assume it so long as it serves their purpose.

In this they sometimes overshoot their mark. A fast man does not desire a fast wife; and officers, who may be thoughtless fellows in other respects, frequently calculate how far their incomes would stretch in the hands of a lively girl who looks upon coins as playthings for the game of ducks and drakes. There is no example of a colonel's daughter failing to obtain a husband if she be nice-looking, sweet-tempered, and modest. The very stillness of her life, contrasting with the riot in the midst of which 'plungers' breathe, is an allurement to wedded blessedness. How often, when racked by a headache consequent on mixed liquoring, a beardless officer curses the dull round of debauchery in which he revolves, like an ass turning a hydrant! He thinks it a beastly thing that he should get fuddled night after night; he recognises the vanity of 'Nap' and loo; he wonders how he can be such a dolt as to lay impossible wagers with Brown and Smith, and to back himself with the cue against 'Cannon' Robinson. If out of the fumes of his late-hour drinkings there rises the face of the colonel's jolly little lass—a girl with no nonsense about her, straight and true as steel—the reflective sub is apt to grow maudlin. Inscrutable Fate ofttimes uses a headache to open the understanding of the plunger, and a night's debauch ushers in a morning of virtuous resolutions, ending in a proposal towards luncheon-time.

When at mess plungers speak civilly of a girl, or when they avoid mentioning her name at table, and only communicate their impressions about her in laudatory terms, whispered in the smoking-room or in private corners, then one may be sure the girl is no talker of slang or taker of five-barred gates. She may be an arrant Flirt nevertheless, for her gentle modesty may be all makebelieve; but she will never be a garrison hack. Plungers are seldom deep enough to see through feminine hypocrisy, and accept a quiet girl's virtues at their apparent worth; but the term of 'hack' is labelled at once on the girl who is free with her smiles, even when she may be in reality much staider of purpose than a more demure minx.

The garrison hack is a girl who has no mother, or whose mother is a weak and foolish person. She becomes fast through ignorance; and grows faster and faster because she mistakes the encouragements of her father's officers for genuine admiration. Her father may not know much about the management of girls, and lets her act as she pleases, without seeing any harm in it. He too mistakes the girl's popularity for a reputation of the proper sort. He is proud to hear men extol his 'Jenny's' prowess in the saddle; he boasts that he taught her early to like horses, and blurts out—good easy man—that he has no notion of a girl's being a milksop. Maybe he frowns somewhat the first time he catches a word of downright stable lingo upon Jenny's lips; but when the novelty of the thing has worn off he pays no further heed, and gets an impression that girls always talked so and always will. After a while he grows so blind to his nice

THE GARRISON HACK.
"Jenny's prowess in the saddle."

daughter's goings-on that he is indignantly astonished and huffed when some elderly aunt or other matronly friend in petticoats thinks it her duty to hint that dear Jenny's conduct might give rise to misconstruction. 'Stuff and nonsense,' says he, 'I'd like to see the man who'd misconstruct—I'd have his ears off!'

A garrison hack's father has never a suspicion of the lengths to which she goes. What he sees is a trifle beside the reality, and what this reality is not a soul knows but the girl herself.

She is a Flirt who has thrown off the reserve of her sex, and a subtle deterioration of her moral sense eventually blunts her perception of right and wrong. It is not enough that she should hunt, dance with twenty different partners at every ball, and encourage men to tell her queer messroom anecdotes, at which she giggles; besides all this, she tipples champagne till her cheeks turn quite pink and her eyes glisten; she lets her fingers be squeezed by her partners, and only makes a pretence of anger when some bold one kisses her in a corner. Where is the harm in kissing? She is not such a prude as to make a fuss about trifles. She thinks she can well defend herself, and so she does; until one day, her heart getting entangled within the wiles of an unusually good fellow, and champagne aiding, maybe, to throw her off her guard, her defences fail her at

the wrong moment. Then consternation follows, and for a week she sobs in private, dreaming of suicide and all sorts of other unfashionable things, including elopement with the seductive aggressor, and love in a cottage for ever afterwards.

But the aggressor always happens to be deep in his tradesmen's books, and unable to afford so much as the luxury of an elopement. He explains this very softly, and consoles the frail one, advising her not to redden her eyes like that, lest other fellows should notice it. Then philosophy ensues. The experienced maiden reflects that hidden faults are no faults, and that her aggressor is an honourable fellow who can keep a secret. He does keep it; and so do others subsequently, one after another, so fast as the careless Flirt treats them to fragments of her love. It is a maxim in such cases that what has been done once may be done again—that one may as well be hanged (if hanged at all) for twenty black sheep as for one white lamb: and the garrison hack's final consolation is that, 'They all do it!'

It may seem to the innocent reader that a startling charge is conveyed in the foregoing paragraph; but it would be a much more startling thing if a girl could adopt the manners of wild boys, mix with them, drink with them, and retain her purity through it all. As well suppose that a full-blown rose could be tossed from hand to hand without losing some of its leaves. Novelists are bound to portray garrison hacks as virgins without spot, but garrison officers know that they are but flesh and blood, which are fragile things. A well-broken hack, however, does not come to lasting grief because she has had a fall or two: this again is one of your novelist's wilful delusions. She takes heart, on the contrary, struggles on, and is never so near to marriage as when her reputation for fastness is so well established that no one can find anything to say against her that has not been said before. A reaction then sets in, and a new set of officers coming to join the regiment, she has the advantage of playing upon chivalrous and unprejudiced young minds, who refuse to believe all that is whispered about 'so jolly a girl.' The newly-joined sub is often an unwary being, and the practised Flirt has little difficulty in alluring him to some pass where the paternal colonel is made to intervene, asking him if his intentions are honourable. There is always hope for a garrison Flirt so long as her father retains active command. Luck only begins to desert her when, papa being put upon half-pay, she retires to some watering-place, and falls into the ranks of commonplace Flirts who, towards the period between five-and-twenty and thirty, fire their arrows at large against all mankind.

There is an old saw as to the kind of men who make the best husbands. It is equally applicable to women. The garrison hack always makes a good wife: tolerant, companionable, and an excellent adviser in difficulties. She has sown her wild-oats, but her husband is none the wiser, for they were sown in the dark.

## The Regimental Flirt on Foreign Service.

Gibraltar, Malta, Canada, and India are all capital places for garrison Flirts. They get a clear field in these localities; for the native ladies can seldom match them, even when they try. Now besides the cavalry Flirt already described, there is the infantry Flirt, who offers two or three varieties. First comes the girl who professes to live in the worship of red coats, and will never marry a civilian. Then the girl who is secretly sick of the army, and would like to catch a nabob, a ship-owner, fur-trader, or something solid of that kind. And next we have the young married Flirt, who is wedded to a marching sub, whose professional advancement she must assist by her affability towards his superior officers.

This last type is common to all professions; but in colonial garrisons the young married Flirt has opportunities not afforded her at home. At an Indian station, for instance, she is often the only pretty woman in the place. Other women there are,

but ugly. The colonel's wife is fat and fifty; the major's is thin and sour; the adjutant has a young wife who gives herself airs, but is mortally plain, and for that reason affects a rigid propriety of demeanour, and takes up her ground as the inveterate enemy of the Flirt. But the Flirt does not care a pin. She is hospitable to profusion, as Indian cheapness in all things but beverages allows her to be; and if her husband's means do not admit of his purchasing unstinted wine and Allsopp, she makes him run up debts. One thing is certain: that her guests never lack for anything, and her drawing-room becomes the regular rendezvous of the garrison officers and the Civil Service officials two or three times a week. It is at once a club, a refreshment-room, and something like a casino. The Flirt sings a little, plays a little, and dances a good deal. She is always ready to let the room be cleared for a waltz. She practises Indian dances with scarves, and the dances of the *Almées*, or rather those plastic contortions which go by Terpsichorean names among the beauties of Eastern scraglios.

The numerous servants that attend upon an Indian household enable a pretty woman to give herself all the graces of a queen. She is worried by no menial work; everything is done for her; she has only to lie on a sofa and command, whilst obedient Hindoos work the punkahs above her pretty head, or brush flies away from her with bunches of peacocks' feathers. Then England and its fashions being so far away, the Indian station belle can improvise fashions for herself, selecting cuts, colours, and

textures which she knows to be best suited to her style of beauty. She comes out in surprising Indian shawls, Chinese silks, light and transparent as muslin, and Japanese satins of heavenly azure blue. At all these experiments in dress—some of them very *risquées*—the other women exclaim, but by and by they pay her the sincerest flattery of imitation; for they see that the men like it, and break out into continual raptures about the Flirt's being irresistibly fascinating, original, and adorable; quite too nice, in fact, to use the jargon *à la mode*.

A beauty who has been plain Miss Brown at home, living in a small villa at Rochester or Southsea, feels on reaching Indian soil as if she had been promoted to a throne. She can do no ill. From the colonel to the smallest drummer-boy, every soul in the regiment is her slave. She has the band to play outside her bungalow when she gives a dinner. She good-naturedly patronises the sergeants' wives; and if a smart-looking private strikes her fancy she gets him promoted. In the matter of leave-giving, punishments, and petty regimental persecutions, she is supreme arbiter; and if a subaltern happens to offend her, he had best exchange rapidly into another corps, for she has quite power enough to crush him like a beetle. No man can guess the might of a regimental beauty's little finger until he has foolishly put himself in the way of being pressed down by it.

The mere fact that a woman should be a Flirt

proves her husband to be a very weak man or a base one. Generally he is a rogue; for there is a something in the honourable character even of a weak man which exercises a moral restraint upon his wife, and prevents her from transgressing given bounds. Or if she be irrestrainable, she goes clean over the bounds ostentatiously and defiantly, leaving her weak lord to maunder or fly into vindictive rages like an infuriated sheep, according to his mood at the moment.

But when one sees a young woman cutting frisky capers under the marital eye, one may be sure that her husband is a creature who makes some profit out of the said jinks; and this is truer in the army than elsewhere. The husband of a Regimental Flirt may not fill his brother-officers with respect; but the world wags very prosperously with him for all that. The debts which he contracts get somehow paid; he never wants a good coat for his back, nor a fine-flavoured cigar, nor a five-pound note for pocket-money. Promotion comes to him rather out of the regular way; and if at a pinch he wants a few hundred pounds to better his social status, the sum is opportunely got on easy terms from a relative of his wife's, whose name she does not mention and which he forgets to ask.

By degrees the creature is dragged up by his

wife to some post of permanent emolument, where he is in a position to crow over other men, his betters. He generally sets up as an implacable censor of morals. He lays the ban of his respectability upon youngsters who have been guilty of boyish follies, and helps to expel such from the service and from clubs 'for conduct unbecoming officers and gentlemen.' He possibly ends by getting to be a general, a colonial governor, or a bank director. So long as his wife remains pretty she is his Providence, and he treats her with proper respect. When she ceases to please he often rewards her for past benefits by beating her or driving her to drink by a systematic course of verbal unkindness, such as only fellows of his kidney can use towards women. Occasionally, if the Flirt has retained her power of attraction after the bloom of youth has gone, husband and wife remain allies till death parts them. Madame becomes the centre of a social circle of strong religious proclivities, and her husband piously leads in the singing of a hymn after a tea-fight.

The Regimental Flirt who is utterly sick of the army might seem to be an uncommon sort of girl; but just as there are ecclesiastical Flirts who are weary of the Church and its ministers, so there are regimental damsels upon whom an overdose of military life has produced the usual effects of a surfeit. This is especially prone to be the case with the daughters of those poor officers who have to pinch themselves and half-starve their families in order to keep up what they call their dignity. A girl of this class can see no fun in the gold lace that costs so much money, and in the taxing duties which bring in so little pay. Even the music of the regimental band becomes odious to her ears, from a recollection of the heavy subscription which is wrung from her impecunious father to maintain it.

Or again, a girl of innate refinement is cast by ill-luck with a regiment whose officers happen to be a raffish set of snobs and churls—pipe-smokers, beer-swillers, courters of barmaids and shop-wenches. The regiment is ordered abroad, and she has an opportunity of taking stock of them all on board the troopship. There, if anywhere, their social qualities ought to come out; but there is not a man among the number whom she can flirt with. At dinner in the saloon, at the daily parade of the men on the fo'c's'le, in the moonlight evenings on deck, the disgusted girl espies their clownishness and lack of wit. She compares them with the officers of the other 'reliefs' on board—some of them nice dashing fellows in the cavalry—and with the naval officers of the troopship, all of them perfect gentlemen, of good manners and great gallantry, and she moans to think

THE REGIMENTAL FLIRT ON FOREIGN SERVICE.

that her fate has bound her to a regiment of such dolts.

The troopship reaches its destination—say Gibraltar—and the boorish lot sink into the same low habits as at home, becoming more offensive, however, in their conceit at lording it on a foreign soil. Then the refined girl falls to hating these officers, and through them the whole regiment, and by degrees the entire army. Bringing her sarcastic powers to bear upon the routine of military life, she decides that the whole thing is a ridiculous mummery; she even doubts the valour of the officers she so intensely dislikes, and thinks she would not trust them to fight in time of war. She says these things bitterly enough in their hearing; she repeats them in the hearing of civilians, which is much worse, and thereby draws down scoldings from her father. Perhaps she has a bout of words with the colonel's wife, who affects to be proud of the regiment, and a tiff with the colonel himself, who growls that, if she were his child, he would have her whipped.

There is no limit to the animosity of a girl who has once given out that she hates the service, and makes a point of inculcating her contempt for it on others. The army has so many detractors among the mercantile classes, whom the arrogance of officers displeases, that a girl of this kind now and then weds a wealthy merchant, on the strength of 'the sharp funny things' she has said about 'those oafs in red coats.' Or she marries a parson. Regimental girls are at all times very much inclined to do that; for to them the quiet parsonages or collegiate cloisters, which certain ecclesiastical Flirts find so slow, are elysium. Nothing enchants the Regimental Flirt so much as to be quit of the atmosphere of tobacco-smoke and pipeclay, which so tickles the senses of her clerical sister. Her dream is of vicarages overgrown with honeysuckle and eglantine; her delight is in choral church-services; and her ideal of a hero generally appears in white cravat and an M.B. waistcoat, if not in a cassock of the new Ritualist fashion. If mankind were ruled by a paternal government, the daughters of clergymen would marry officers, and those of officers clergymen, and the world would possibly be happier than it is just at present.

## The Seaside Flirt.

There is a girl who, living in a remote country place, goes to the seaside for one month in the year. Of course, during that month of comparative bliss she flirts. But all through the rest of the year she does no flirting even by letter. So, albeit to her seaside acquaintance she may seem a Flirt, yet it is obvious that flirting is only her recreation, not her business. She is no more a Flirt than a man who occasionally pops at a sparrow is a sportsman.

The true Seaside Flirt lives by the sea. The half-season is her harvest-time, when there are a few visitors to notice her, but not enough to eclipse her. In the full season there are balls, races, concerts; in the half-season there is—flirting. A ride upon the sands, even on the backs of ill-saddled donkeys, may easily be turned into an imaginary ride for life. A shrimping excursion, besides offering chances for a display of neat ankles, brings about solitary wanderings, two by two, among the rocks. A sail in a small boat in rough weather affords opportunities for the exhibition of nerve and nautical knowledge combined;

while a fishing-party by torchlight leads to so many nice things in the way of huddlings together under one tarpaulin, little screams when the boat rocks, delighted exclamations and joint action when the fish is speared or netted, that the mere mention of it will set any acute girl blushing.

Should the place be a port, the landing of foreign cattle may be construed into danger, and may be made

THE SEASIDE FLIRT.

the occasion of a gallant rescue; or an injudicious attempt to swim at bathing-time will perhaps challenge the bravery of the other sex. Here it may be remarked that the foreign custom, which puts men into bathing-costumes as well as women, has its advantages, if only this one of allowing the rescuer of a fair swimmer to carry his lovely burden on to the beach in sight of an applauding crowd, which cannot well be done arrayed as Englishmen are at present when they bathe.

There is no little circumstance which a clever girl will not convert into a chance for flirting. The well-timed loss of a purse or a dog in the place where our lone damsel is a stranger, a dispute with a fly-driver, the loss of a hat in a high wind, a sudden sousing from a too boisterous wave, or the dropping of a handkerchief over the pier-railings, are all little difficulties that may be turned to account: 'So silly of me—so good of you: really I ought to have some one always by my side to take care of me.' 'Lucky some one!' 'O, you're joking; but really I'm ashamed to have given you so much trouble.'

The paradise of a Flirt, though, is a yacht. No horrid billiard-room to take up the time of the interesting man; no need to run away from cigar-smoke in the exhilarating fresh air. Frequent meals, and gay; frequent nips of liqueurs, or mulled wines, to keep the cold out, and prescribed as indispensable to

health; and then the privilege of appearing to lose one's balance, and needing the prop of a stalwart arm. No visible impropriety either if the proprietor of the stalwart arm does hug a little in conveying the fair and unsteady one to a seat. Add to this that Etiquette, which would be shocked at seeing Miss Jill and Mr. Jack walking up and down an hotel corridor for an hour at midnight, can look on unmoved at a moonlight promenade on the deck of a yacht, even when it extends pretty far into the small hours. Life is a chain of inconsistencies.

The one-month-a-year Flirt has a keen eye for the names on the visitors' list of the seaside town to which she resorts. The odds are that she discovers on it some man she knows—her brother's friend, or the son of papa's friend—anyhow, one with whom she has flirted before, and whom she describes as 'the only man who can wrap my scarf comfortably round me on this bitterly cold beach.' This paragon she ferrets out and catechises as to what he has done since they last met. She is sure he has been flirting, and lectures him about it, saying it is high time he settled down soberly, as she herself thinks of doing. Thereupon she walks her truant off to see some dear, interesting, gossiping old sailor. If he did not go with her, she might not find the man: does he mind being seen so often walking with her?

When a young friend is engaged to be married, the Flirt eagerly becomes her chaperon, knowing that her male acquaintances will rally round her more quickly while she is protecting the fair flower. And when the Flirt is again alone, she keeps very close to some old gentleman friend in a Bath-chair, sometimes carrying on a flirtation with him, for want of better material; sometimes using him as a convenient escort.

Our friend, thanks to an iron constitution, which

the month of ozone-breathing develops finely, does more execution in the daytime than in the evenings. She is not quite enough informed about arts, sciences, or London tattle to shine in conversation, nor sufficiently accomplished to dazzle by her music and dancing. Her circumstances do not enable her to compete in dress with ladies and nymphs of the 'great world;' but her powers of sustaining a fatiguing walk, row, or ride; her ready flow of small talk, and quick sympathy, make her a delightful companion wherever the proportion of gentlemen to ladies is about three to one. It is only when temporary helplessness looks pretty that she assumes it; one of her favourite sayings in merry company being, ' Wherever there's fun going I'm your man.'

Poor girl! she does not get quite as much fun as would be good for her; for when her month at the seaside or on board a yacht is gone—and how fearfully quick it goes!—she feels in a sad way while packing up her boxes to return home. One more year's pleasure past, and another twelvemonth's dulness to come. It is only a cynic who would grudge this interesting occasional Flirt the amount of enjoyment she can squeeze out of her four weeks' annual trifling with the strong sex.

There is another sort of Seaside Flirt, who is found more often on foreign coasts, and in the smaller towns thereof, than at Brighton or Scarborough. She is the daughter of somebody under a cloud.

Her father or perhaps her brother has gone to the dogs. She finds it pleasanter not to live in England. She has no taste for purposeless travelling, and soon establishes herself in some quiet watering-place such as Fécamp, Tréport, or St. Valéry. She has sense enough to conquer her first impulse towards utter seclusion, and to select a place not *too* lonely; possibly she will go so far as to select Dieppe; but not Boulogne, which has too bad a name. She has given her address to a few friends, and some few more may find her out. But she is aware that a large number of her summer friends will never ask for her again, and she is resigned.

This girl has perhaps not been a Flirt in England. Staid old country ladies had been her valued friends; gentlemen had respected her highly; some had been intimate with her, but she had not cared for flirting, nor encouraged it. Flirting is tame between old family friends, and it was among these that she lived.

But coming without introduction and alone with her mother to a new place, the desolate English girl has new habits to contract and new schemes to form. Her acquaintance now is among the ephemeral passers-by. Men are struck with her beauty and

with her air of melancholy, which she tries in vain to throw off. They cannot get at her history, which, of course, heightens the interest in her. They find her infinitely more agreeable than the empty-headed milliner's lay-figures which they are accustomed to meet at such places; and if by chance some portion of her story leaks out, the pity of the men silences the tongues of the women who would rail against her. So, by degrees, after one man has innocently asked for her home-address, that he may have the pleasure of renewing his acquaintance with her, and another has told her that he prolongs his stay in the place solely on her account, and a third has owned that a neighbouring seaside town has more attractions in the way of scenery, but not (with a bow) such company as one meets here, the fair exile insensibly yields to the temptations of flattery, and, finding that every one expects her to flirt, turns and drifts with the stream.

It is virtually a question of flirt or sink. She fears that by avoiding company she would confess to the intense shame she feels at the disgrace that has fallen on her family. She also recognises that, having no longer a chance of getting married through family influence, she must secure an establishment if she can, by her own sole charms and accomplishments. She sits and works at some piece of tapestry, as the French ladies do in the local assembly-rooms, while the band plays of an afternoon; she attends Sunday services at the British Consulate; she is always superlatively neat in dress; and she remarks that she can play the most difficult pieces of music at sight. She is very assiduous at cultivating her French; it may some day be the only language that she will have the opportunity of speaking. Yet she does not like France, and would not settle there for worlds, so she thinks. 'O, those Frenchmen! such figures!' she owns, laughing, to an English adorer,

'Why, Marquis! you are looking younger than ever.'
'Yes, truly, it's an old habit of mine.   I'm Conservative.'

and they quiz the Gaul in company. The adorer is young, and has a tawny moustache. He speaks low, and looks into her eyes whilst addressing her. He seems to know nothing of her history, and alludes to a pleasant country hall and park which he will inherit when his uncle dies. For the present he has only an allowance of 500*l*. a year; but he knows a friend who married upon that and got on famously, because his wife loved him and made a little money go a long way. Does *she* know how to husband money? 'Let me look at that ring on your finger,' breaks off the adorer suddenly, and adds that it reminds him of one which his mother used to wear. The ring is held out, and the little hand with it. Adorer inspects both, and gives a squeeze. 'O!' exclaims the fair exile, pink and agitated; but a peddler, offering polished pebbles for sale, interrupts this idyl on the beach, and the proposal which was starting to the adorer's lips is adjourned till the morrow.

Alas, before next day somebody has been at work saying something, and the adorer has vanished. He has not even gone through the formality of forging an excuse for his departure, and saying good-bye. He has decamped, as though he had had a narrow escape of a great danger. Exula does not cry, but sets her lips and perceives that there is a gulf thenceforth between her and the land of her birth. She makes sure it was that odious Mrs. Black, with the ugly daughters, who circulated her story. Mrs. Black cuts her next time they meet on the parade; young Black, with the eye-glass, remains faithful to her, but has the impudence to wink as he accosts her. Young Brown, too, a fellow with orange whiskers and a good heart, tells her that the women are abusing her like pitch, but that he doesn't care. She packs Black and Brown about their business. No more English company for her. She is too sensitive to brook slights, and too proud to accept sympathy; she will not stoop either to the degradation of going to mix with other proscripts at Boulogne, where none would dare cast the stone at her. She and her mother change their residence, and repair to a town wholly French, where they commence the process of entirely denationalising themselves.

Exula changes her religion. She and her mother go to mass and make friends with the parish priest, who comes sometimes to dinner. They have French servants; read French newspapers; and give up corresponding with England. Their piety gets talked of in the town, and the priest gives out that they are fervent Catholics who have left their Protestant country because they could not practise their religion in peace there. Every Frenchman knows that religious persecutions are still rife in Queen Victoria's dominions.

By dint of prudence, propriety, and paying their way regularly—by dint also of the unsuspecting priest's good offices—the two Englishwomen collect a little coterie of French friends round them. The girl is too pretty not to excite attention. She accepts invitations to *thés*. She consents to show off at the piano, and sings some English ballads which become the rage. Her French improves apace, and she can understand the compliments of red-trousered officers, as well as bandy chit-chat with young *rentiers*. However, marriage is a business in France, and before any Frenchman commits himself to an offer, inquiries are made through the priest as to the amount of *dot* which the 'belle Miss' possesses. The intimation that she is living on an allowance which may or may not be continued after her marriage thins off a number of candidates. Not but that several young men of twenty-five and thirty would be content to marry her without dower did their papas and mammas permit it; but their papas and mammas will not, and according to French law they have power to prohibit.

There remain some men past forty. The English girl touches them wonderfully by her enthusiasm about France. There never were such men as Frenchmen. So much politer than the men of other countries—so much wittier, braver, and more companionable. The literature of France is delightful, so are its climate, wines, theatres, cities, boulevards, and the dresses of its ladies. The English girl says she is dying to learn how to dress like Frenchwomen, who have a *je ne sais quoi* impossible for foreigners to catch. The gallant Gaul assures her that she has quite seized that *je ne sais quoi*, and completed it with a touch of English grace and piquancy. The time comes when the exiled girl sees that one at least among the middle-aged wooers who say these things sincerely feels them. He is fat and bald, but he has 600*l.* a year, which looks bigger because he calls it 15,000 francs of income. He evidently thinks it a fine competency too, for it enables him to live in greater comfort than an Englishman with twice the money. He has a country house which he styles a *château*, a garden which he terms a park; he is mayor of his village, and a knight of the Legion of Honour.

Such *partis* are not to be caught every day, remarks the priest the day before the man of forty's maternal uncle comes to pop the question in his

nephew's name, for Frenchmen think it bad taste to go through this formality in person. One may be sure that the maternal uncle lays great stress on the fact that his nephew asks for no *dot;* such disinterestedness seems to him to savour of mediæval chivalry. He says that the notary will draw up a contract in which mademoiselle will have a suitable portion settled on her. Mademoiselle's mother thereon accepts, and mademoiselle herself fixes a day when she and her ripe betrothed shall be introduced to all their friends assembled for the signature of the abovesaid contract as an affianced couple. After all, this is a better ending than many other exiles can pretend to. The English girl who in her own country should marry a fat man of forty, of dubious lineage and having but 600*l.* per annum, would not be thought to be doing well for herself; but circumstances and lands alter cases.

## The Tourist Flirt.

The Flirt who has failed to find a husband during the London season may recruit her health in travelling for a fresh campaign, and perhaps pick up what she wants into the bargain. In foreign hotels marriages are arranged as frequently as in London drawing-rooms.

But the tourist season is more suitable to the married Flirt than to the girl. The latter, held in bondage by her family—accompanied often by a cohort of brothers and younger sisters—and inclined, for prudence sake, to be more demure abroad than in England, stands at something of a disadvantage towards the married Flirt, who looks upon touring as a period of complete liberty. She may have her husband with her, or may be travelling alone with her maid and a *dame de compagnie;* perhaps her husband is dead, or perhaps he has ceased to care for her jinks—in any case the married Flirt, being removed from the control of prudish English eyes, plunges with delight into the freedom of *incognito*

existence. As her objects are not similar to the girl Flirt's, she has not the same reasons to be particular. It matters little whether her neighbour at the *table d'hôte* be eligible as a husband since she has no thought of marrying him. So long as he is agreeable, gallant, enterprising, she can get out of him all the fun she wants. In this way the married Flirt picks up *cavalieri serventi* wherever she goes—

to-day a Frenchman, to-morrow a Russian Prince, next week a Wallachian shiny with hair-oil and diamonds. She has a smattering of all languages, or, at least, can understand a compliment in any tongue.

To some of these married Flirts autumn travelling is really the most pleasurable business. Look at the pretty blue-eyed Englishwoman who steps out of her hotel on the Rhigi to watch the sun rise on a crisp September morning. She is wrapped in a fur cloak to keep the cold off, and a polite Italian with moustache who stands beside her arranges its folds, and lends his arm that she may steady herself on the rocky ground. She had never seen that Italian before yesterday, when he sat next her at the *table d'hôte;* but it turns out that they are both

THE FROZEN CORPSES AT THE HOSPICE ST. BERNARD.

going the round of Switzerland, and it is tacitly agreed that they shall go together.

Why not? There is no spoken convention on the subject, and they do not drive up to the station in the same cab, nor, on arriving at their destinations, repair to their hotel in company; but they contrive to travel in the same railway carriages, and in the different hotels where they alight their rooms are often contiguous. One week you may find them at the Hôtel National of Geneva, whence they proceed on steamboat trips about Lake Leman as far as Ouchy or Vevey. The week after behold them at Lucerne or at Berne, sauntering together under the arcades of the picturesque old streets, or feeding the bears in the municipal bear-pit. But suddenly there is a dissolution of partnership; for in another few days our married Flirt turns up at either Ems or Homburg, but this time with a Bavarian Count to escort her when she goes to drink the waters.

The German watering-places have much declined from their gaiety since the gambling-tables have been closed; and those who go to them in the hope of finding any vestige of the old revelry are disappointed. Ten years ago they were the casinos of the plutocracy throughout Europe. Now they have become the resort of a good many people who positively require the waters for purposes of health, and whose Bath-chairs are not an enlivening feature in the gardens of the Kursaals. Nevertheless, the beautiful scenery remains, and the bands of music, and the attraction of an occasional crowned head,

who comes with a large suite, and causes crowds of aristocratic families to come also.

The married Flirt at Ems will possibly find it

convenient to declare that her health is delicate. Her physician has prescribed her the waters that taste of steel, and she must mind and take two hours' walking exercise every day. These are fine opportunities for the Bavarian Count. By a happy coincidence he is always loitering near the ferruginous spring when the lady comes down at eight, at noon, and at 4 P.M. to take her drink. He passes her the

goblet which the German attendant wench hands up brimming with the tepid stuff; he laughs with her at the grimaces she makes; and then when the jorum has been gulped down he is ready to attend her in her walk at a quick march through the gardens, or out into the country among the woods and fields of maize. As all this whets the appetite, the

Bavarian is delighted to see how his fair *England-erin* tackles the viands and wines at the hotel dinner. The Italian might not have been so pleased, for men of his nation like to see a woman feed herself with pastry and *confetti;* and perhaps that was why she parted from him. Honeymooning in Germany requires that both should be of one mind about eating.

Besides, eating forms one of the chief resources of flirting. On the Mediterranean steamers that ply between Marseilles and Civita Vecchia, and thence to Brindisi and Alexandria, the Flirt, freshened by the salt breezes, makes her four or five meals a day; and half the time of her lovers is spent in fetching her ices or glasses of sugared water on deck between whiles. For you can get ices on board these Mediterranean boats; and when the blue sea is calm as a lake, and the sun not too hot to prevent the passengers from sitting under an awning, the Flirt finds it not disagreeable to relieve the trouble of returning answers to foolish questions of the soft sort by trifling with one of those many-hued blocks of Neapolitan ice which look like soap.

However, even the Mediterranean is apt to tumble about; and in such rough conjunctures all continental gallants, whether Frenchmen, Bavarians, or Greeks, dive hastily into their cabins, leaving the English tourists masters of the deck. The Englishman is not very prone to sea-sickness, and for this reason makes a better maritime companion to the Flirt than any other. Being adventurous, too, he will, perhaps, prolong his acquaintance with the lady who has struck his fancy at Brindisi by accompanying her to Egypt, where they steam up the Nile together as far as the second cataract, and do the Pyramids on their way back. Everybody knows that doing the Pyramids with a lady involves nothing less than lifting her continually in one's arms, to assist her ascent from stone to stone until the platform on the summit is reached. There are, to be sure, black Nubians, whose business it is to do this for money; but the tourist who would win a pretty Flirt's regard will not surrender such delicious labour to hirelings.

## Country-house and Town-house Flirts.

'What is all this smoke about?' 'O sir, it's Miss Louie, who got on to the roof last night with Mr. Tom, and stopped up all the chimneys with old newspapers.'

Miss Louie is a Country-house Flirt, who delights in playing practical jokes with her cousin Tom, or with anybody else who may be handy. She thinks nothing of clipping up a hair-brush into the bed of a bachelor guest. She makes apple-pie beds for crusty old gentlemen, judges and suchlike; she muffles up the clappers of bells; puts aperient waters into the tea-urn; and paints the tail of a Countess's pet Havannah sky-blue.

The Countess happens to be a Flirt too—a *grande dame* too high placed for scandal to assail her. She abhors practical joking, and preaches to Louie—a sort of connection of hers—on the utter bad taste of the thing. Louie does not care. She puts on a comical pout when being lectured, and delights to plague the Countess above all other women. Why?

Because the Countess is what Louie calls an arrant poacher, for ever trying to appropriate unattached men, who are not fair game for married women.

Louie is nineteen, but looks younger. She would have got married two years ago, but for practical jokes played upon suitors who had serious intentions towards her. Wishing to try the nerve of one, she took a loaded gun from his hand, said, 'Mind your eye,' and shot both barrels over his head, within an inch of his hat. He swooned with fright, and Louie laughed till the tears ran out of her eyes. Another suitor was bragging of his horsemanship. Louie defied him to ride a donkey of her own, which she alleged to be as tame as a lamb; but she had sent Tom to hire a vicious Nubian jackass from a strolling circus; and when the horseman had bestridden this beast, it carried him through a quickset hedge, where he left much of his clothes and portions of his skin. He did not forgive his *inamorata* for the intense mirth with which she hailed this exploit.

Louie likes no one except Tom, whom she plagues as much as others, and who often calls her a 'little brute.' There has been no talk of marriage between them. Tom would hesitate proposing to a girl who might sew up his coat-tails on his wedding morning. She, on her side, has no present thoughts of matrimony. She likes flirting too well. She flirts with everybody; deliberately leading one man after another to believe that she is in earnest, and then coolly enlightening him as to her real sentiments by some joke, which sends him away besplashed with ridicule and gnashing his teeth. Louie is very pretty, and can assume all sorts of manners. She can sham sentiment, melancholy, deep corroding love; and she once nearly drove a simple silly lover frantic with terror, by saying she would die for him, and flinging herself into a lake with her clothes on. She can swim; and when she scrambled out remarked, laughing, that she had tried the water-cure for love, and that truly it had cured her.

Louie does not like London, though she has spent two whole seasons there, and beguiled her weariness as she could by decoying the Countess's lovers from her. She was the Countess's visitor; and my lady had to threaten more than once to send her home. There is no describing the pitch of secret enmity to which these two arrived; and if it had not been for the fear of what Louie's malicious tongue would say were she packed off, her ladyship would have broken with the girl once and for ever.

For the Countess is one of those ladies for whom life is love and love is life. She has a husband, but never troubles herself as to his whereabouts. They

are occasionally together, when they are good friends enough, unless the Countess happens to be troubled with one of her nervous headaches, which make her waspish; but at ordinary times my lord goes his way and my lady hers. Twenty men at least, among the best in society, have, turn by turn, acted as the Countess's *cavaliere servente*, attending her in all places, and having their *petites entrées* to her boudoir; but, as we have already said, she is too high perched for scandal to touch her. Who has a right to complain if her husband does not? She changes lovers almost as frequently as a jockey does horses. Every man who is for the moment a 'lion' in society becomes the butt of her shafts; and many of these lions, succumbing, have had the honour of being led in her train for a week or two like pet spaniels. She has tried all sorts of men: poets, painters, warriors, statesmen, and foreigners. An Italian and a Hungarian fought about her with pistols; a Frenchman and a Spaniard exchanged blustering epigrams in her honour. The very effrontery of the things she says and does closes the mouths of people who would criticise her if she were more timid. Nobody believes ill of her, because if people believed anything at all they would have to believe too much.

Such a monitress as my lady might have converted madcap Louie into a Flirt of the finest brilliancy, and she conscientiously tried her best for the girl whom she befriends for family reasons. But Louie — like most practical-joking maidens — has money of her own, and does not care whether she is

befriended or not. At any rate, she claims to go her own way, and that way is not the Countess's.

Perhaps she divines more about her chaperon's goings on than she ought to be able to do if girls were as innocent as novels paint them. She has uttered a queer thing or two at times, which have made the Countess's ears tingle, and turned her lover for the nonce to the colour of mulberry. 'My dear, you must weigh your words,' her ladyship would say, biting her lips. 'Why, if there's nothing in them they can't hurt you,' was the pert response.

Girls like this Miss Louie have their uses, for, Flirts themselves, they can divulge all the tricks of their craft for the amusement of ears masculine. They are the spies and traitresses of the women's camp. For the sake of raising a laugh they will blow up secrets like so much loose powder, and they are the first to tell men that the saintly purity, the angelic sweetness, the virginal modesty ascribed to women and girls are all 'bosh.' Louie has before now entertained her cousin Tom with recitals of the conversations she used to hold at school with other girls, and there was the grin of semi-incredulity on Tom's lips at the enormity of these conversations. When reproached for her flightiness by those who have a right to reproach her, Louie usually says, 'O, boys will be boys; why shouldn't girls be—boys too?'

Flirts of Louie's temperament make good wives for hypochondriacal men, who may be the better for a little healthy excitement; and, on the whole, it may be said that the man who marries a Flirt at all had best wed a merry one.

## The Sentimental Flirt.

Until arriving at the age of twenty-five the girl of sentimental mood is only a quiet uninteresting maiden, with a strong bias for poetry, chiefly of the modern school, that will not scan or construe. She has an album, and collects autographs; she writes verses, and has drafted the plot of a three-volume novel, not written; she despises this age of money. One day she wakes up and reflects that woman was not made to live alone. Many of her old school-friends are already wives and mothers; and in the numerous novels from Mudie's which she peruses she notices a tendency to depreciate the matrimonial chances of virgins who have reached her time of life. Her poetical instinct warns her that there is no romance in old maids.

So she rouses for the fray and puts on war-paint. A fine figure and carriage, a well-trained intellect, a strictly conventional manner, a good family connection, a few art-treasures as heirlooms, a domestic taste underlying her keen poetical sympathy with wives of the Guinevere pattern—all these things might combine to make her an excellent wife for a man of easy temper, not addicted to claim autocratic powers in the home circle.

But Lavinia—as we may call her—is beset by difficulties caused by her peculiar temperament, nourished on Tennyson and Browning, and fortified by Swinburne. An average man will not do for a damsel who feels a deep contempt for men who have not, like herself, set their faces against a mercenary age. Lavinia's husband must be in some twenty respects superior to all other women's husbands. He need not be rich or noble; she would, on the whole, prefer that he should be neither, so that he might not dwarf her with his superiority. But he must have every sort of physical and intellectual advantage, co-operating to make him a glorious compound of mind and matter. He must be handsome and modest, fascinating and faithful; able to knock down an ox one minute, and tenderly to fasten a fallen earring to his wife's ear the next. He must be peaceful, yet firm; an artist, orator, sportsman, statesman; a hero of land, sea, or balloons, yet never bored by small-talk; a *savant*, without being a pedant; well dressed, but not extravagant—such a man as never was, even in books, and, alas, never can be.

But Lavinia believes in his existence, in her power

THE SENTIMENTAL FLIRT.

to find him, in her ability to discover merit which before was hidden. So she draws out, examines, and criticises all her male friends. Of female friends she has only one, and into her ears she pours her plaint. The poet is sickly, the dragoon fast, the divine slow, the merchant ignoble, the baronet a *roué*. Not one may marry her; and at last, by dint of disenchantments, she grows sour, except to her canary, and hates men almost as much as she detests married women. But she sketches miniatures with pen and pencil of the man she could have loved, and these much resemble the wax presentments in barbers' windows.

The Sentimental Flirt, after a period of misanthropic retirement, often takes to literature, and flirts with authors. She submits a copy of her verses to the Laureate, and, getting a polite reply, is emboldened to try a work in prose. While the book is going through the press she has an exciting time correcting proofs; but disillusions await her when the critics fall to flouting her heroes and heroines with ridicule. Her second attempt is not so trashy as the first. She aims determinedly at success by a story of conjugal impropriety, which strikes one of the most sensitive chords in the breasts of habitual readers of novels; and though this second book gets a lavish share of abuse, it elevates its authoress to a distinct position in the world of letters.

Then she begins literary and epistolary flirtations with publishers, editors of magazines, brother authors, and foreign translators. She defends the moral scope of her works in letters to the reviews, and develops a thesis of her own as to a recondite meaning of the Seventh Commandment. She mocks at British prudery, and says to herself that genius was ever venturesome. She puts a bust of Byron in her study. Surprise is created among the public when it becomes known that the authoress of so much 'spice' is not an experienced widow, nor a lady living on a pension earned by long service in the 'half-world,' but a lady of good connections, still young, and strictly virtuous. Strictly virtuous women of a sentimental turn often astonish the world by the depth and range of their knowledge.

But perhaps the Sentimental Flirt has taken to charity, instead of literature. In this case she becomes a distinguished member of the Society for the Protection of Animals. She busies herself about the grievances of dogs, cattle, and cats; she founds a home for motherless kittens; she bans the barbarity of foxhunting and game-shooting, and has serious ideas of inquiring whether the owners of racehorses cannot be brought to punishment for causing their nags to be unduly flogged. For men she does not care—at least, not for Englishmen; but she will gladly start a fund to relieve Turks, Bulgarians, or Cossacks, because she conceives them to be animated with sentiments more romantic than she has met with in her own country.

After all, our highly-cultured Lavinia is not proof against the blandishments of heroes of the Corsair type, and she becomes less and less proof against them as she grows older. Towards her thirty-second year she starts on a tour for Italy, and nearly leaves her reputation in the hands of a seductive Sicilian brigand, with a sugarloaf hat. She takes to painting, and gets Neapolitan lazzaroni to pose for her. One of this set becomes her servant, a strapping dark-eyed fellow, with merry white teeth, whom she calls Beppo, and who answers her in a fondling whine, addressing her as 'Eccellenza.' She, perhaps, marries this creature, and soon after has to advertise in the papers that she will not be responsible for any debts which he may contract in her name.

Or, instead of marrying, Lavinia falls into anxiety about her soul, and embarks in spiritual flirtations with monks and plump Italian priests. She goes to Rome, and signalises herself by dropping on her knees in the streets when religious processions pass; she kisses the toe of St. Peter's statue; she requests an audience of the Pope, and has a fit of hysterics in the Holy Father's presence. Her rotund monkish friends

and still more rotund priestly advisers encourage her to give largely of her substance to conventual establishments; and during a week or two she wonders how she would herself look in a nun's habit. If it were possible to dress in white, with a scarlet cross and cape, she thinks she would take the vow; but the white-and-scarlet Carmelites happen to be a rigidly cloistered order, whose regulations would not suit Lavinia's taste. She would like to walk about the streets in nun's attire; but, seeing that the nuns who walk about are robed in hideous blacks and grays, she eventually gives up the idea.

Possibly Lavinia's impulses towards religion and self-sacrifice one day branch off in a Mahometan direction, and lead her into an Egyptian or Turkish seraglio. Lady Ellenborough is not the only Englishwoman by many who has discovered that romance, though banished from the rest of the world, still finds a refuge in the breasts of Mussulman cheiks; nor does the polygamous system rebuff, for a cheik who takes one gushing English spouse soon finds that he has got as many wives as he can manage.

## The Studious Flirt.

Before taking leave of our subject we have a few words to say about the Studious Flirt.

The woman who is truly scientific is not a Flirt. The genuine frequenter of the Round Room of the British Museum, of the South Kensington picture-galleries, or the lectures of the Society of Arts, would no more favour the advances of the male sex than would Pallas herself. But every true article has its imitations, every flower its parasites; and though the firmly-rooted wallflower of the National Gallery or of Exeter Hall would doubtlessly shrivel up like a mimosa under the male touch, yet the parasites, who are not truly studious, but only wish to seem so, behave very differently. Indeed, they too readily avail themselves of the opportunities which their pursuits furnish them to carry on their flirtations in the most open way.

Young men, pushed by circumstances into learned society, may meet with young women dragged thither by relations; or desperate Flirts may even repair to

THE STUDIOUS FLIRT.

these meetings on their own account, to hunt down the men who are too shy to show themselves at wedding-breakfasts and similar matrimonial marts. And there are few things easier than to beg prettily for an explanation of that little difficulty which Indocta can never understand without a guide, but which Studiosus of course knows thoroughly how to explain.

An excuse being thus found for half-hours of conversation in which the chaperon takes little part, the down-hill road is safe and pleasant. Sometimes an old book-grub is sooner captured than a young one, both as being less on his guard and also as being less closely watched by the dragon aunt who generally presides over the destinies of studious young men. But woe to the damsel to whom the literate old gentleman uses the words 'my dear'! They mean that he is married long ago, and can be nothing to her. Even if widowed, those who say 'my dear' to a girl seen for the first time, seldom care to marry twice.

There is a Studious Flirt, who really has no pretence about her. She has received an education of a very learned sort, which has early filled her mind with a taste for science. She is, perhaps, the daughter of a professor or archæological lecturer. She began to assist her father in correcting proofs when she was sixteen, and by the time she was twenty she had learned to take a serious interest in

his pursuits. At her father's suggestion she tries her hand at an essay, which gets printed in a magazine. It treats of 'Woman's Dress in the Middle Ages,' and gives proof of observation and historical research. The style is, of course, loose, and the affected use of learned words makes the article read somewhat ludicrously to the critics. It gets 'whipped' in consequence. The young lady bites her lips, but rallies. Her next contribution to the press is couched in a more serious vein, and secures for her a few compliments from the critics. After this, Miss Studiosa gets formally admitted into the ranks of the learned.

She dons a double eyeglass, and lets herself be elected an honorary fellow of an Archæological Society. Accompanied by her father, she joins summer excursions into Cornwall and Wales, where cromlechs, funeral tumuli, and vestiges of Roman camps are to be found. She carries a reticule, into which she drops bits of flint, which are supposed to be arrow-heads and lance-heads of the Age of Stone. She becomes a connoisseur in antediluvian remains, and you could not deceive her about the precise age of a broken earthenware pot excavated from a sand-pit.

But archæological excursions may lead to flirting. Those young professors in spectacles are often sly fellows, who can wink in stray corners, and convert the inspection of an old bone into an occasion for saying soft things. Studiosa is not made of wood, and listens kindly to the compliments that are paid her. For all that, she would rather flirt with a dragoon than with a *savant*, because woman likes to assert her superiority, and there is no possibility of doing this with a man who knows more about bones and tumuli than she does.

But perhaps Studiosa botanises. In this case there are many fine days, when she can exchange soft nothings with young gentlemen interested, like

her, in collecting ferns and orchids. She wears a tin box slung to her side. She stoops to find rare specimens of vegetation growing in rocky nooks. Some of these are out of her reach, and she requires assistance to climb up to them. Studiosus, fresh from Oxford, lends her a hand or a 'back-up.' Between them they succeed in uprooting the rare vegetable. Studiosa, in consigning it to her tin box, says, 'So kind of you!' Studiosus answers: 'There is nothing I would not do for you.' After which he tries his tongue at a compliment: 'I wish I were that fern.' 'Why?' 'Because it is next your heart.' 'O!' says Studiosa, and slings the tin box round to her right side; but she has blushed, and Studiosus is half caught already. If she will only be kind to him during the rest of the botanising trip, he will make her an offer of marriage at the moment of separation.

Studiosa, however, may go in for abstruser subjects than archæology and botany. There are many free-thinking young ladies in these times. They have read Darwin, Renan, Herbert Spencer, and Huxley. They have made up their minds that this is an age of shams; that religion is an error; and society, as at present established, a delusion. They sneer when they pass churches; they contribute to atheistical publications; they think that marriage is a civil contract, and that sensible people should never have the nuptial knot tied in a church.

Studiosa, as an atheist, is sure to be an awful

person, and will either not marry at all or will marry a curate after she has repented. Men do not much care to have free-thinking wives; but a pious curate, falling in with a comely infidel, may haply try to convert her, and render himself very interesting in her eyes by so doing. He will speak so softly that Studiosa will be touched. She will have learned by this time that science is vanity, and that the reading of Darwin brings no spiritual consolation. She will hanker after church services, and dream of getting married in a church in regular bridal attire and with full choral service. If she have a little money the curate will propose to her, and they will make a great fuss together about her taking the Communion for the first time, and thereby sealing her abjuration. Learned young ladies who have forsworn religion are generally most anxious to have their reëntry into the fold affirmed in the most solemn manner possible. If Studiosa could have her way she would, when marrying the curate, have all Darwin's and Renan's books burned at the altar.

ON H.B.M.'s SERVICE.

## I.

### Introductory.

A YOUNG man with a handle to his name, and who has an inborn talent for doing nothing agreeably, may find the British Diplomatic Service as pleasant a profession as he can select. Other people find their way into it, but are never quite at ease there. Diplomacy, in our time, can hardly be called a serious business, out of Russia. Formerly, Austria and Germany had some important negotiations, relating to dynastic questions, always going on at foreign Courts; and their Ambassadors were often consummate masters of the difficult and delicate art of pleasing wisely. Now an Ambassador has no field for action. A pair of permanent clerks connected by an electric wire manage all his official affairs; and whenever any event in the country where he resides arouses the smallest public attention, a lynx-eyed company of newspaper correspondents take the blush off his news, and put him to shame with it.

A modern Ambassador is not even allowed to be bumptious. He must eat the humble-pie offered to him, with lowliness and thanksgiving, if steadfastly minded to keep his salary. For, should he make any noises whatever, the local Government laugh him to scorn. They do not dream of wasting words on him, as the courtly Ministers of a bygone age were wont to do, when an Ambassador's dignity was held by international lawyers to be identical with that of the Sovereign whom he was supposed to represent. They merely set on foot a notable plan for obtaining his recall by private letters. Confidential notes having reference to his alleged backslidings are frequently exchanged between influential personages; and as a host of rivals have been waiting for his Excellency's discomfiture ever since the day when his appointment first appeared in the *Gazette*, they soon get wind of his misfortune, and make an ugly rush at him, so that he is speedily brought to naught. A very small knot of people closely tied together really govern the world just now; an Ambassador must contrive to form one of its threads, and to remain tightly bound in his place, if he expects to lie safe and snug.

A supple-backed colourless person, who observes the conditions tacitly dictated to him, will have no cause to complain of his lot while his connections are in office. The principal posts in the service are handsomely paid; several noblemen and gentlemen have been known to receive from seven to ten thousand pounds a year, with a liberal margin for contingencies, though it was sometimes thought that they would hardly have earned so much for themselves in law or medicine, which are, nevertheless, better paid than most professions. A friendly Secretary of State, boldly backed up by the permanent officials in his department, has, indeed, several ways of making things pleasant to an Ambassador in whom he truly delights. Outfits, travelling allowances, secret-service funds, are all nice comfortable things in their way when discreetly managed; and they are entirely at the disposal of strong-minded public servants, who cordially sympathise with each other.

One bold British diplomatist, who was but a modest Envoy in rank, very good-naturedly received a hundred and odd thousand pounds in a few months from the sources above mentioned; and his accounts were enough to make most persons wink, when permitted to look at them. The archives of the Foreign Office are, however, so discreetly preserved, that few indeed were the individuals outside the department who had any occasion for winking at these sublime figures. Another worthy man, who gave highly-respected dinners on returning to his native land, brought 700,000*l.* home with him as the fruit of his prudent negotiations; and this solid addition to our national wealth would have promptly founded a peerage, and remained with us in a legislative form to this day, had not its possessor wandered with it into foreign stocks and got lost.

Now if mere Envoys thrive so prodigiously as to become Envoys Extraordinary indeed under favourable conditions, how (ay, how indeed?) may not an Ambassador flourish when properly fostered and sheltered while raising the wind? One of them, who practised the invigorating trade of a pawnbroker during the piping revolutionary times which sent the Imperial house of Bonaparte flitting, got several fine estates into his hands, and a curious collection of house property and jewelry, at extremely moderate prices. He has been highly respected ever since.

The romantic East is still the real gold-field of

DIPLOMATISTS IN THE ROMANTIC EAST.

diplomacy. Very big things indeed are sententiously dropped into the pockets of Ambassadors, who calmly hold them open and—gaze upon the stars, absorbed in contemplation too lofty and ethereal to remark a sound so mundane as the chink of coin. The business is quite religiously contrived when an experienced Ambassador once gets into the knack of it. A large grant of land in a populous city for a church or a cemetery may be converted into hard cash with a piety almost affecting; and a shrill wife has often increased her stock of family diamonds, in an altogether surprising way, merely by early knowledge of a Court scandal before it was bruited abroad. In one case a Royal abdication, kept secret, under diplomatic guidance, till the latest moment, gave rise to some very spirited transactions in the regalia, while the treasures of the local church were disposed of at such reduced prices that a Cabinet Minister recouped himself for losses in Canadian railways by a discreet speculation in them.

Of course the resident diplomatists, who were earliest in the secret, made a still more delightful thing of it. Ambassadors have often had cheerful windfalls of this sort in recent years; and the intelligence of a national bankruptcy, which happened within living memory, was as good as the daily discovery of a gold-mine, as long as it could be kept dark. One fine honest fellow made 200,000*l.* sterling out of it in almost less than no time; thereby demonstrating, in an engaging and pleasant manner, how becoming and nice a thing it is to be a friend of one's Prince.

Persons of quality, with the fine breeding of exalted station about them, do not pass each other money-bags from hand to hand, as vulgar people do; they rather take an opportunity of presenting money's worth to gentlemen and ladies in good society who are of use to them, with the assurance of their perfect consideration. This method of standing in for a valuable thing is altogether more decorous and polite.

Most of our Ambassadors were poor men on starting in life. One of them used to tell how he lived in his gay youth over a pork-butcher's, and dined off a biscuit. After his demise his personal property was estimated for probate as only just under 400,000*l.* None of them have ever been heard of in connection with any money scrape after returning from an embassy. Perhaps it is a law of Nature that they are miraculously endowed with large bankers' accounts in their mature years. Perhaps it is the nature of our law so to provide for them. Perhaps of all public men they deserve best of their country; for we are never called upon to hear their speeches, and the true bent of their genius lies in cookery.

## II.

### AMBASSADORS.

A few years ago there were only five of these august creatures going about on the face of the earth as representatives of the majesty of Great Britain. One started in his ennobling life as a lawyer's clerk; one was a Scotchman who married a title; and the other three were titled born. None of them had ever written, done, or said anything remarkable, or they never could have risen to their conspicuous eminence—for promotion came slowly to all of them. Even the Scotchman spent thirty-seven patient years in climbing to the gilded rank of Excellency. The way to promotion was, of course, made easier to the persons of title; but even the most popular member of the greatest ducal family of the governing Whigs could not do the ambassadorial thing in less than twenty-two years. Indeed, it must be thoroughly well known and understood by all whom it concerns—and their name is legion—that there is nothing in a man before he is honoured with the most brilliant reward in the public service. Lord Dalling was the last person of real ability who was appointed English Ambassador, and he has had no successor. Indeed, candid politicians in the confidence of Government admit that he would never have obtained such an honour save by a miracle, and never have kept it under any circumstances but for the fortunate chance that he happened to be an invalid, who was nearly always on leave of absence, and who was steadfastly believed to be upon the point of death.

The place of British Ambassador at a foreign Court would indeed be intolerable to any man of average energy and mature intellect. He has no power of initiative in any business; and his public conduct is absolutely under the control of telegraph wires, which are for ever instructing him, night and day. By his own countrymen he is considered as a peg on which to hook complaints. The courtiers of the country where he resides treat him with civil scorn if he gives himself airs, and as a Jack Pudding if he does not. The Ambassadors of Russia, who are intrusted with real powers, and are commonly the intimate personal friends of their Sovereign, feel an unfeigned contempt for him; and the Ambassadors of other constitutional States regard him as a fellow-actor in the performance of a heavy farce, which has ceased to attract public notice. In truth, the Ambassadors of constitutional States have an un-

comfortable sensation that they are all pretending to be what they are not.

The worst of their business is, that even foreign

princes and potentates, who used to give our Ambassadors a friendly hand now and then, and help them to go on shamming with their august support, are now frightened out of their wits at the sight of them. Ambassadors such as the first Earl of Malmesbury and the late Earl Granville actually did possess a good deal of Royal and Imperial confidence, which was useful upon occasion; but King Clerk's dishonest trick of printing the private conversations of monarchs in Foreign-Office blue-books, abominably edited, has closed such sources of information; so that a judicious prince, who meets an Ambassador by accident, shuts up his mouth with a snap, as though there were a steel clasp to it.

A deal of envy has been expressed in news-sheets and elsewhere about the preference given to titles over merit in the diplomatic service. Titles, however, make a goodly show in all Courts, while they are still more favoured in Republics. A very small lord looks larger and more important in the esteem of rich and idle societies than a very great philosopher. This fact being indisputable, however moralists may carp at it, no Minister should be lightly blamed for taking it into account when making his promotions. A lord will do far better for a lay-figure than a man of genius or a man of business; and, as it is now universally acknowledged that Ambassadors have no rights and no duties, dull empty folk with sounding names can fill, with peculiar decorum, so meaningless an office.

A fat man, in a fright, too, seems to run away from danger with more haste and anxiety than a large-minded and thoughtful statesman having serious feelings as to his responsibilities and duty towards his fellow-countrymen. It is quite refreshing to remember the alacrity with which his Excellent Plumpness the Right Honourable Bickerton Pemell Lord Lyons removed himself out of harm's way at the public expense during those alarming riots in Paris a few years ago, leaving, with perfect taste and an unruffled temper, the Queen's lieges to take care of their own interests. Nobody missed the noble and energetic gentleman who had rolled so fast away from peril, and who was far more at his ease when beyond danger than while exposed to any possible mischance. Excellency Lyons, his cook, and his quarter's salary, rejoiced in safety and quiet all through a noisy war which convulsed the Rue du Faubourg St. Honoré; and they were a thousand times better situated than that American, Mr. Washburne, who looked after his fellow-countrymen in the besieged metropolis of France, for less than a fourth of the pay awarded to the high-souled Englishman. Indeed it is a comfort to recollect that our represen-

tative, during the whole war, prudently kept out of all broils but those of his own kitchen, where he and an imaginative cook held sympathetic council together over succulent meats and appetising sauces.

Such a man was, and is, an honour to his native land. Let us rejoice in him.

There seems to be no certain rule for mounting to the topmost round on the ladder of British diplomacy. Men as brave and unselfish as Lord Lyons have tumbled off from unexplained causes. Each step is made by the help of patronage, and therefore depends on luck. A perfectly colourless well-behaved nobleman, who has been brought up by an experienced mother, holding a good place behind the scenes of the political stage, will always have a nice chance, if he and his mamma live long enough to make use of their friends and experience. She will teach him to be patient and courteous; never to tread on anybody's toes or heels; never to be eager, or apparently desirous, of promotion, till even rivals and competitors cry out that his professional advancement has been fairly earned.

When he means to move on he should go, as it were, sideways rather than straightforward. Big posts are best got by jumps in zigzag directions, so as not to do violence to the jog-trot notions of secretaries of legation, more than sixty years old, yet full of hope in the remote future. If an aspiring young fellow and his mamma tumble over the heads of some of these old boys they make an awful hubbub. It is a good plan to pop in and out of the Foreign Office, to get brief spells of special service, to have something to do with a Royal Commission, and yet never to be seen or heard of in a newspaper, unless in connection with an extract from the *Gazette*.

It used to be said that attachés appointed to the smaller Courts had most luck, but of late Fortune seems to have changed her haunts. The youngest of our Ambassadors, Lord Odo Russell, began his career as a subordinate at Vienna, and ended it at Rome. Lord Augustus Loftus passed eight years of his early life in the remarkable retirement of Stuttgardt.

There are few Ambassadors on the pension-list, and their retiring allowances are not large, considered as the ultimate end of so much ambition and such vaulting hopes. They are generally lords, however, poor old souls, if that is any consolation to them; and they cost the nation, when lumped together, no more in superannuation doles than half, or maybe a third, of the yearly earnings of a country solicitor in moderate practice. Possibly they really want nothing.

They are great lights at their clubs, these frail and worn-out wrecks and spars of forgotten vessels, freighted with forgotten schemes, that have gone down in the ocean of time. They are in earnest request at christenings and weddings. Their names are thought to look well in the trust-deeds of marriage settlements; they are often fished for, but seldom hooked, by promoters of public companies; for they sink heavily into silent pools, like large tench, as soon as they have carried off the bait held out to them. They may be met in fashionable neighbourhoods during the season, strutting grandly home-

wards, with feeble knees, from pompous dinners, where they have been the honoured guests. Their orders and decorations are firmly sewn on to their dowdy dress-coats by the hands of loving women, who firmly believe that they are the centre of the universe, round whom all other men are in duty bound to revolve. They have small select companies who admire them fervently once, or even twice, a week, over weakish tea, and who listen to the favourite stories of their youth as to the oracles of a prophet.

Now and again they ask a question in the House of Lords, or propose to ask a question; for experience has long ago taught them not to be too hasty, lest they should get into some difficulties with the

Ministry about their pension, or about some sly old job in hiding, to which they are fondly attached. They spend weeks in preparing this 'question,' till it becomes quite a marvel of antiquated official jargon, utterly incomprehensible to the human intellect. Then if it is a fine day, if Ministers look benign, and the rheumatism permits, they go down with their excited womenkind to Parliament, and have a fieldday all to themselves. They utter, in a jaunty quivering chirp, a few sentences about the old, old story most familiar to them—the Eastern Question, the designs of France, or the views of Germany towards the sea. Presently they are beckoned and coaxed and petted and whisked away by the worshipful women in time for their five-o'clock milk. The rest of their

evening is passed in revising proofs of the wonderful speech, which has been transmitted in manuscript, through their confidential man-of-all-work, to the editors of the morning papers, 'with Lord Protocol's compliments.' The editors perhaps privately ejaculate 'Bosh!' but print it nevertheless, as in a manner bound by the custom of their craft and country.

Sometimes Ministers, when hard pushed, will even galvanise one of the awful old boys back into real life for half an hour, and call him up to make an authoritative statement, or denial, or warning, or prophecy in the interests of Government, sending him back with the 'Garter,' or some grand sham of that sort, for his trouble. His name as a politician reads to the general public, at such times, like a quotation from ancient history, producing, as it is intended to produce, a truly grand effect in the way of universal bewilderment.

Such poor counterfeits and shadows as herein described are modern Ambassadors. An embassy still seems sometimes to be what it has often been before—a sort of stately almshouse or retreat for decayed politicians; sometimes also it is a convenient shelf on which to lay a dangerous rival, and make him at once harmless and contemptible. The late noble Marquises of Thormanby and High-down-Derry were both neatly extinguished in this way—

the one by a Tory Minister, the other by a Whig, for no party has a monopoly of the tricks of the trade in politics. The only question, however, which now concerns the sane part of mankind is whether Ambassadors would, could, or should be something better than they are. If they would be, perhaps they could be; but when a weak-kneed mortal has been for a long time laboriously climbing against wind and weather to the top of a steep hill, he seldom feels much inclined for heroic exertion. Sleep and a glass of sherry are often more suited to his mind. Probably he takes the sherry before the sleep.

The idea of 'should-ness' or duty suggests quite a different train of thought. An Ambassador who had conceived a thoroughly healthy notion of his position and its proper functions might prove a very valuable factor in this world of ours. He could hardly do so much as Manchester men suppose for their immediate trade profits, because a commercial traveller, with a pushing disposition and a quick head for figures, can see clearer into small mercantile gains than a ripe statesman. But he might so patiently study the history, manners, circumstances, and government of the country where he is accredited as to make any misunderstandings about her strength, finances, and resources impossible. Under our present system of patronage and nepotism, an Ambassador was the immediate cause of the Crimean War, of the Franco-German War, and of the Turco-Russian War of 1877, whereas an Ambassador might have prevented all these calamities.

In like manner a few far-sighted reasonable men would have known enough of the resources of Egypt, Turkey, Spain, Greece, and the South American Republics to warn off rash trust in them, and to have prevented the widespread ruin it occasioned. They would at all times be able to forecast some of the probabilities of the proximate future, and to show where an investment in foreign securities would be prudent or otherwise. Trustworthy and timely information is always beneficent in its effects; and to a wise Ambassador, who made a right use of his opportunities, mankind might often owe the discovery of new wealth, new truths, new forms of happiness. It should be his especial work to discourse with men of science, to follow and examine their experiments, to share, as it were, in their discoveries, and to watch the precious fruit of thought and labour till it became ripe. It is melancholy to think that the first idea of the electric telegraph seems to have died stillborn in the mind of a poor mechanic, that many valuable and beautiful arts have perished unpreserved, and that there are still specifics favourable to health and life known to obscure savages and village crones, but unknown to our physicians.

A thousand thousand secrets of Nature remain unrevealed to us for want of intelligent inquiry; and every country has curious mysteries unexamined. Is the ordinary practice of medicine right in France or in England? They are often directly opposed to each other. Which is the best code of criminal law? Nearly every nation has a different one. Why is Chinese agriculture much more productive than ours, while the soil and climate are less favourable? How came it that Macadam imported the art of road-making from Pekin, and not Lord Macartney? It had been known in China for centuries; and Macartney was there till 1794, whereas Macadam's discovery was not made public till 1819. What are the secrets of colour known to the carpet-makers of Turkestan and to the shawl-weavers of Persia? How do the Arabian jugglers perform their marvels, such as to make a tree grow, blossom, bear, and wither in an hour, and recall dead snakes to life by music? What is the miraculous stone of which Sir Patrick

Colquhoun heard tidings at Corfu? What says the horse-whisperer of Aleppo? Is there any virtue in the hazel-rod of the well-finder in Southern Russia? What is the drug which cures all disease, but death, in Tartary? It is administered by an untaught peasant, and nobles, long past physicians' skill, resort to him in numbers, and are cured. He will take no money. Is it true that the mineral wealth of the Ottoman Empire would pay her National Debt a hundred times over?

No Ambassador deals with such questions as these, or is likely to do so, as matters are at present constituted. Suppose we tried a different sort of genius. Not to speak of living men, what an Ambassador Franklin made! What an Ambassador Sir Humphrey Davy would have made! And if we could have persuaded Henry Holland, who was fond of travel, to join him for a year as medical secretary; and Erskine, when he first turned his mind to the law! He would have been glad of the place of first legal attaché, instead of living a rough and tumble life with his wife in barracks at Minorca. What a flash such an intellect would have cast into the darkness and muddle of our legal procedure, with experience so widened and improved—had clerkly meddling permitted! James Watt, too, who had an uphill fight with the world when young, might have made a figure in this sort of diplomacy, just about the time when he was allowed 'by especial favour to establish a small shop in Glasgow.' He and David Brewster would have told us all something of the 'properties of light' worth hearing; and would have made together such an embassy as never left the shores of England.

We prefer another mode of doing business. We take a dreary old fellow with a handle to his name, send him to a foreign Court, and pay some clerks to exchange rigmarole with him. Then we despatch another dull or dullish man, who is to know nothing of that rigmarole, unless called upon temporarily to take the place of the first old man. These two poor creatures are called the Ambassador and the Secretary of Embassy. They are seldom on speaking terms; and employ such mental energy as they have in writing viperish private letters about each other. 'D—— that pompous duffer! he never goes on leave,' murmurs the Honourable Daddleton or the Honourable Babbleton. 'Why, hang it all, if I were to go away for a day only, Doldrums' (the Honourable Babbleton's or Daddleton's nickname) 'would see my "*most secret and confidential*" despatch about the royal footman's startling revelation concerning the Queen's new shoes; and he would get at my best source of information,' mutters Ambassador Faddleton, who is a lord, of course, or nearly of course. 'Quite right!' observes Lady Faddleton, in an uncompromising tone; and henceforth Daddleton or Babbleton and the Right Honourable Lord Faddleton sit watching each other, and hatching petty social mischiefs.

The small fry are at it too. The military attaché, who is a general (goodness knows how or why), feels permanently aggrieved because Daddleton or Babbleton takes precedence of him as Secretary of Embassy. The other attachés are jealous of each other. Weedesby is 'my lord's favourite,' and gets all the special service. Beadsby is consul and librarian, which means pickings; and Deedesby sulks twice a week at a tavern dinner with Babbleton or Daddleton, both being in a state of private revolt against things in general. Their conversation is not interesting to other people. Hyejincks, Shycock, and Crasshe, all golden youths belonging to the first families, patronise the local amusements, and call several actresses by their Christian names. 'My lord,' however, smiles at their doings, for he is somehow in the grip of Shycock's father, Sir Underwood Shycock (firm of Shycock, Downey, Dodger, & Co., of Lombard-street); Hyejincks is Lady Faddleton's nephew; Crasshe is Lord Bango's son, and Bango is Secretary of State in command at the Foreign Office.

Hyejincks, Shycock, and Crasshe are mostly on leave of absence, save when a new play or a new loan is coming out.

## III.

### Envoys Extraordinary.

An En. Ex. and Min. Plen., as he is officially designated in that great work of genius the 'Foreign-Office List,' may be called the ordinarily successful or working man of business in diplomacy. A steady presentable fellow, who goes stolidly in for the thing; who has money, or knows how to make it silently, and give it to the right people, is tolerably certain to become an Envoy Extraordinary and Minister Plenipotentiary towards the shady side of middle life. If he is really in the confidence of influential people, and can put the screw on them, he may even jump into a mission at a single bound, though the thing does not often happen nowadays, because persons who can weigh heavily on Ministers of State employ their power more advantageously: for no place in the diplomatic service, as at present constituted, is worth the attention of a man of energy, talent, and character.

There are a good many active bustling fellows among our Envoys, who are not quite so much impeded by dignity as Ambassadors. The best of them,

however, seldom find anything to do since the telegraph from Downing-street became so confoundedly communicative. Even the man in Persia, who used only to be worried by a Gholaum, or orthodox official courier, once every ten days, and was never expected to answer a despatch in less than six months, is now teased among his kabobs and rose-trees whenever any permanent person in charge of the wires feels naughty.

The people at Pekin, Yedo, and even Tangier, which a few years ago slept so pleasantly amidst her orange-gardens and happy hunting-grounds, are troubled as sorely. They are perpetually being bothered to give explanations, and to furnish reports, and to answer

long lists of printed questions for some unholy compiler of statistics. It would not much signify if the messages were all delivered in a bundle, or rubbish-basket, once a week; for their contents are of no consequence, save that they put the recipient to a little unnecessary annoyance, and generally to some needless expense. But unfortunately they are left separately at the Minister's house in the small hours, by special favour of the local authorities; and the sleepy diplomatist is often obliged to start up from his slumbers to read them in his nightcap, lest they should contain tidings of import, such as his abrupt dismissal, or promotion, or transfer to another post.

The social position of British Envoys, too, is much altered for the worse in our day. Thus the 'T. G.' or travelling gentleman, as the fine old British tourist was good-humouredly called at the legations thirty years ago, when he came out with a special passport, a travelling-carriage, and a suite of honour, carried his welcome with him. He was generally a man whose good word was worth having on his return to England, and it was expected that he would bring the latest scandals from the clubs and the cover-side. The 'T. G.,' therefore, had scarcely arrived at his hotel before the Minister's butler, who was rather an august person, brought him a verbal invitation to dinner, which he was expected to answer verbally.

He had good cause to brag of that dinner all his life afterwards, and generally did so. The Envoy was a truly splendid and magnificent creature, far above butchers' bills. He kept open house, and not only dined admirably, but his recognition immediately gave the T. G. an entrance into good society. The best political news and the most amusing stories current were to be heard at his table, and every one who was worth seeing or knowing in the country could be met there.

No part of the national taxation was more profitably spent than that which went to keep up the splendid hospitalities of such men as Stuart and Ponsonby, Normanby and Temple. To be on pleasant and easy terms with them was part of a liberal education. Now penny news-sheets and parliamentary riots have awakened tourists to the uncomfortable knowledge that diplomatic salaries are of small account in a banker's book unless eked out by serviceable wits; so the moneyed interests feel rather contempt than respect for a wiggy old boy in a foreign town, who cannot give them half such a good feed as the manager of the branch shoddy-shop, who is flourishing in the most fashionable part of the city, with a brace of friendly cooks, and a music-hall songstress for a wife.

Several Envoys, too, who have scrambled into uncertain places through money-lending attorneys, and have been a good deal fleeced in the process, are in no haste to discourage an idea which spares them the obstreperous visits and undisciplined appetites of virtuous engineers prowling about with their capitalists, on the look-out for foreign contracts leading straight into the Central Criminal Court. A modern British Envoy, thus overwhelmed by travelling bagmen and cheap excursionists of every denomination has given up his time-honoured part of entertainer-general to his fellow-countrymen. He is now rather a diner-out than a dinner-giver; and his saucepans often have rest for a week together. Rich local merchants, ambitious people struggling for a place in polite company, thriving shopkeepers eager to buy manners, are always glad to have a diplomatist in leading-strings if the thing can be accomplished on remunerative terms, and the man is a decent sort of fellow who does not assume too much consequence.

The financiers and large usurers in great cities like Paris, Vienna, Berlin, and St. Petersburg, usually invite their diplomatists in batches, so that one may see all the powers of the earth represented at Herr Schnapsgeldt's Sunday villa. The smaller capitalists, who have made but half a fortune, take them in turns, one or two at a time. They are mostly harmless old fellows, even over their cups;

being chiefly remarkable for hair-dye, stiff neckerchiefs, and a steady faculty of digestion. Idleness and small fixed incomes, free from every care but the telegraph, endow them with a regular appetite every day at the usual hour fixed by the social customs of the place where they reside. They become rare judges of other men's wines as they grow in age and wisdom.

The wit and grace, the geniality and good-fellowship, which brightened the missions of Howden and Holland, Ellis, Heytestury, and Seymour, have died out of the service. Lord Bloomfield was the last of the cheery old school.

## IV.

### Secretaries of Embassy.

Mr. Jenkins Bathurst Jenkinson-Jenkinson is a fair average type of a Secretary of Embassy. There is a tradition in his family that one of them was the great-aunt by marriage of a personal friend of the second Earl of Liverpool; and they have all wisely claimed noble lineage ever since. Thus it very naturally happened that when Lord John Bustle, who had a great respect for the peerage, was in power at the Foreign Office in 1852, he appointed Jenkins first paid attaché to the Paris embassy right off.

'The Lord deliver us from this dreadful Whig!' gasped Mr. Hammond, when he saw the nomination lying in wet ink on 'Littlejohn's' own table. 'Who would have thought that so small a creature had such monstrous notions?' Then it was rumoured that Mr. Addington objected to instruct the chief clerk of the period to make out the appointment of Mr. Jenkinson, it being against all precedent.

Now, Mr. Addington was at this time permanent Under-Secretary of State; and Mr. Hammond was the senior clerk who governed him, and the chief clerk was a highly respected three-bottle man, who had been at the battle of Waterloo.

Such a combination of official malcontents, and the fact that they had a candidate of their own (bound under conditions to pay an annuity upon his salary to the chief clerk), would have staggered any Secretary of State but Lord John.

'You will witness stranger things than this, Mr. Hammond,' squeaked his lordship, in that highly-pitched voice which so long tried the gravity of the Strangers' Gallery in both Houses of Parliament: 'I mean to make myself an Earl, and *you* a Privy Councillor, before long; you see if I don't.'

Indeed, Lord John Bustle carried out both these intentions; but the Office was not to be appeased, and ultimately triumphed even over the godfather of the Reform Bill, so that the chief clerk's customer for promotion had to be appointed after all, instead of Jenkins. That favoured young man did, however, contrive to wriggle edgeways into the diplomatic service, and was smuggled off to a half-forgotten Court in Northern Germany as soon as the usual negotiations were completed. He did not, upon the whole, come so badly out of the business, for the harmless necessary attorney who touted for the Foreign Office agent reported favourably of him, as a discreet

THE HARMLESS NECESSARY ATTORNEY.

young man with a still tongue and his aunt's savings, who was likely to leave his salary for an indefinite period in his agent's hands without asking questions about it. From that time forward, therefore, Jenkins was considered as a safe person, who might be officially mentioned on every change of Government as 'a rattling good fellow, who had been doocidly ill-used by Timbertoes in Lord John's time.'

For Timbertoes was the endearing name by which the Waterloo officer, who had been chief clerk, was familiarly known; and since his decease all the musty peccadilloes of the department have been laid at his door.

Mr. Jenkinson would have got on faster than he did in the service, but he committed two capital blunders at starting. He failed to secure the good graces of his chief's wife, through dancing with and paying too marked attentions to a bankeress, who was her rival, at the first Court ball given after he took possession of his post; and he committed the unpardonable offence of shirking attendance on her at shopping; for he was but a lad, and inexperienced in the ways of his profession. Sir Phipps Ryder, who was head of the mission, took a grip against him at his wife's bidding, as was natural and proper; so that Jenkins had an uneasy time of it till he could afford to be transferred by the attorney to another post, where his chief was a bachelor.

Here, however, he fell into a trap of a different sort; for, being determined to please the Envoy at any price, he made himself so accommodating that this diplomatist took himself off from a courtly residence somewhat dull, and left his subordinate to manage the mission business at his own expense. Mr. Jenkinson-Jenkinson's savings were wofully dimi-

JENKINS AND THE BANKERESS.

nished by these proceedings; for he did not dare to touch his salary, even when promoted to the rank of paid attaché, in consequence of further arrangements with the touting attorney, made through a shrewd old uncle. Moreover, when Mr. Townshend Fox-Robinson, his new master, found out to what good service a docile chap like Jenkins could be put, that worthy gentleman did all he could to obstruct his subordinate's professional advancement, for fear that some domineering young nobleman, without a rap, should be sent out to him in place of the mild convenient Jenkinson, whom he had learned so well how to appreciate.

This little game went on for six weary years. Poor Jenkins got a gray hair with the miserable thought that he might be ruined for ever by being forced, in spite of all his sacrifices, to draw upon his official pay in his agent's hands—a course which he had been warned by the touting attorney would ruin his diplomatic prospects for ever. Just as Mr. Jenkinson-Jenkinson, however, was about to sell out his last thousand pounds in the Funds, which was all that remained of the slender fortune he had inherited, honest Lord Malmesbury came into office, and, having an inkling of the Jenkins case, quietly shelved Mr. Townshend Fox-Robinson; after which he transferred the long-suffering attaché to Constantinople, where the whole embassy staff were just then handsomely boarded and lodged by Colonel Rose—afterwards Lord Strathnairn, the famous Indian hero.

At Constantinople Jenkins was lucky enough to

LORD TRUFFLETON HANDING JENKINS HIS APPOINTMENT.

obtain employment on special service, which brought him into contact with a dowager Earl, then cruising about the Ægean in his yacht. This illustrious legislator, finding that the aspiring diplomatist could make an omelette of tomatoes better than his own cook, offered him free quarters for ever, in a moment of culinary enthusiasm; and Jenkins might, on the whole, have passed a more useful and agreeable life had he taken service with the amiable voluptuary rather than in the Foreign Office. But he could not be brought to understand so plain a truth till too late.

His lordship (Earl Truffleton), however, was not vindictive, and good-naturedly ordered his own confidential solicitor—a prince of the law, who lived in Bolton-street, Piccadilly—to negotiate with his professional brother, the tout, to get another step up the ladder for Jenkins. A fortnight afterwards, which was just the time required for return of post, Truffleton almost took his young friend's breath away by tossing him his appointment as Secretary of Legation in Switzerland, on handing him a basket of fresh eggs to prepare for breakfast.

'Of course,' observed his lordship, 'you can't go to Berne. I never do. I shall want you here till October, when the equinox will drive me home by rail through Trieste. I will get you transferred to Naples by next year. There are excellent tomatoes at Naples. You may run and see your friends while I winter in Paris.'

'How about leave?' asked Jenkins dryly, being somewhat puffed up with his new dignity, even in presence of the patron who had pitched it to him so scornfully.

'Leave!' answered Lord Truffleton, too much astonished to swallow the mouthful of good food he

'BARKER, MY LAWYER.'

had just taken before speaking. 'Barker, my lawyer, could transport your agent and head man at the F. O. if the dog dared to interfere with my breakfast; and, by George, he should do it, too!'

Mr. Jenkinson-Jenkinson paid marked attention to this powerful peer for the rest of his days; but unfortunately he did not live long, or there is no knowing how high he might and could and would have pushed a young fellow who could handle a frying-pan so deftly, and who so truly pleased his taste. His lordship's conversation was most considerate. 'Much better stop with me altogether, Jumper,' the peer was wont to insist, having given his friend a nickname derived from the accomplished manner in which he tossed the materials for his lordship's favourite breakfast. 'I will give you three hundred a year, damme! and your livery—I mean, my man Davis can make your clothes. Pension too, when you are too old for work.' It did not occur to Lord Truffleton that he would ever become old.

'You see, Jumper,' his lordship would shrewdly observe at other times, when urging Jenkins to enter his employment, 'I can afford to be liberal. My ancestors did all the thieving and that kind of thing for me, and my family have been honest for two generations. Your present masters, on the contrary, have all their thieving to do, and will flay you alive before they have done with you. My noble friend Furby, though he ought to have money, if he has not been bullied out of it, is worse than any of them. My place is worth more than anything in the public service—except the F. O. agencies, and you'll never get the tip of your finger into that pie. Come, is it a bargain? No? Ah, you'll think better of it to-morrow.'

That to-morrow never came. Lord Truffleton died quite suddenly, choked by a grapestone, while laughing over one of his own jokes after dinner, at Venice. Jenkins was, of course, in attendance on him, and sincerely expected a legacy; but the kind-hearted Earl could never bear the thought of any one but himself, and naturally departed this life intestate. Immediately after this fact transpired Mr. Jenkins was dryly recalled to his diplomatic duties by telegraph. He never again met with such a friend as Lord Truffleton; but Naples was one of the best posts in the service, till spoiled by Mr. Gladstone; and as soon as Jenkins was Secretary of Legation he now and then got a spell as Chargé d'Affaires. Many easy-living English people of influence also resided in the most beautiful of the Italian cities; and Jenkins had opportunities, which he eagerly seized, of rendering them small services, knowing from experience how good a thing it is to be on pleasing terms with the aristocracy.

At length a wealthy Italian Duchess, who had two British and one Wallachian husband, all living, wanted the place of Secretary of Legation, near her

own marine villa, for the first attaché, a rosy young fellow, aged twenty-five, whose society she considered unusually edifying. Finally the great agent, Mr. Cribb, finding that Jenkins had honestly kept faith with him, and had already left eight years' pay in his hands untouched since the last accounts between them were settled privately in Truffleton's time, was really disposed to befriend so conscientious a customer. Mr. Jenkinson, therefore, was half-intoxicated, half-alarmed at receiving, quite unexpectedly, his promotion as Secretary of Embassy at Berlin, which is the dullest post in the service.

He was exhilarated, because it was a tremendous jump upwards; such a bound as must make him Minister Plenipotentiary *ad int.* very shortly, if he could only keep it during a temporary eclipse of the Ambassador. But he was also alarmed, because the slippery place of Secretary of Embassy is often an awkward stepping-stone to some abominable frying-pan in South America. There was even a horrible tradition of a Secretary of Embassy having been once shipped off as Consul-General somewhere, and that so much against his will that he died of a broken heart. These were grim warnings; and Mr. Jenkinson-Jenkinson henceforth devoted the entire energies of his diplomatic intellect to keeping out of sight and out of mind. The close of his career, like the beginning of it, will depend entirely on chance.

## V.

### SECRETARIES OF LEGATION.

The Honourable Peregrine Villiers Timmins is a demure colourless man of [forty-three, who never had a friend or a sweetheart, lest either should interfere with his professional prospects; and therefore

he is Secretary of Legation at Copenhagen. There is likewise talk of sending him to Yedo, as soon as young Melgund-Stanley can be coaxed or scolded away from Paris, where he is anxious to espouse a lady of gallantry older than his mother.

Hartley and Beaudesert, brilliant Jack Canning and gifted Philip Goldsworth, who started in life with Timmins twenty years ago, have been all distanced in the race. Lord Fairflower, too, threw up the service when he came into his family estates after the death of his uncle; and Everhard Bullion, the banker's son, thought he could do better for his firm in Parliament, or with the Prince, than as old Protocol's right-hand man at Vienna. Perhaps he was right, perhaps not; but these and other retirements, jobs, and resignations, which had taken place during a score of years under six Secretaries of State, had gradually cleared the coast for the Honourable Timmins; and there he is perched, like one of Mrs. Carey's chickens half-way up a lighthouse, and never likely to get much higher in this world. He has two sets of shirt-studs, a collection of dress-boots, a doubtful diamond which belonged to his grandmother, and a miscellaneous assembly of clothing from all nations. That, with five hundred a year in salary and four hair-brushes, represents the sum-total of his possessions under the sun; if a pair of rather frightened whiskers and a false tooth can honestly be left out of the calculation.

The mental baggage of Timmins might be stowed away in a wonderfully small compass. He has often read in *Burke* and *Debrett* that he is the fourth son of Conway-Lenox-Montague-Petty-Thynne-Dunk-Fitzroy Viscount Nocashingmore, of County Tipperary; and nothing has yet occurred to disturb a belief so advantageous to him in society. That is, almost nothing; nothing save an after-dinner conversation which he once had with the present Viscount, when he declined to back his lordship's bill of exchange for a hundred pounds, and was consequently disowned by that august nobleman with much promptitude and asperity. If the truth must be told, the late Viscountess (heiress of Sloe, Twiggs, & Twiggs, the great tea-dealers of Pudding-lane) had separated from her husband very shortly after her marriage, and had allowed him an annuity to let her alone at Florence. But that is an old story now, and need not be recalled.

Besides, it is not, perhaps, all true; for the Honourable Peregrine is often pleased to relate anecdotes of his early life, for the edification of the counts and barons who strut about at the Court where he resides; and from these artless narratives it is clear that Timmins must have passed the greater part of his infancy and youth in circumstances or extraordinary splendour. Most of the continental papers call him 'cet illustre fashionable, Milor Teems,'

and stoutly assert that he owes his title to a share he possesses in the *Times* newspaper, which, as all erudite foreigners are aware, is held by the Lord Mayor of London and his more powerful vassals, upon feudal tenures. Timmins has often found it amusing, and even profitable, tacitly to encourage this belief; so that there prevails an opinion among three French milliners and a German governess established in the Danish metropolis that he is a personage of no small importance. He would think so too, if he did not get so awfully snubbed by his master clerk at the Foreign Office, who is angry with him for not paying tribute with a mind sufficiently zealous and a hand open enough.

In truth, Timmins does not find his salary too much for his own uses, and he will have to struggle all his life with pecuniary embarrassments, as his viscountly namesakes and possible progenitors have done before him. His chief will never budge for a week from the Swedish dominions, so that he cannot get hold of the allowance of three guineas a day which would be granted to him if placed now and then in charge of H.M. Mission.

Then Sir Hookham Backhouse, K.C.B., her Britannic Majesty's Envoy to the King of Denmark, has been saving candle-ends any time these thirty years. He will never ask any one to dinner except on the Queen's birthday, and then the dinner is a bad one. Thus, upon the whole, the position enjoyed by the Honourable Peregrine Timmins, for which he is envied by one-half his contemporaries and despised by the other, is hardly a satisfactory one if fairly examined. The Danish Royal Family would rather he was richer, and that he made things better for trade at Copenhagen. The Danish nobles wonder why he does not entertain them; and the Danish ladies are partly surprised and partly indignant that he never dances with any one who is unmarried, also that he dances somewhat awkwardly, as one whose purse is over-light, while his heels are over-heavy.

The great prize of a Secretaryship of Legation, so coveted by attachés and consuls, is like some other worldly splendours, and will not bear looking at too closely. Timmins got it by a fluke, having been employed to make a shabby sort of secret report for the purpose of whitewashing a man at the Foreign Office who had blundered into a hot-headed scrape from over-bumptiousness. In the end he got the place of the man he had libelled, and brilliant George Beaudesert was hustled out of the public service. The smallest creatures do the work which God appointed for them often quite unconsciously; and Timmins, who may have privately owned to himself that he was a contemptible sort of chap, who had gone backbiting for hire, was merely an instrument in the hands of Providence to teach a great soul patience, and to lead it into higher regions of thought and contemplation than those which are bounded by a despatch-bag.

## SECRETARIES OF LEGATION. 201

Timmins got his small reward, such as it was—125*l*. paid quarterly or not, as he happened to be in the good graces of the clerk who governed Lord Furby. Once, when that terrible travelling Countess Mawley was displeased with him for not capping her courier, 100*l*. was deducted from Timmins's salary all in a lump; but he got over it; and recently there has sprung up a report that he is about to be married to the large Baroness Schochchild (*née* Hedges), one of his mother's kindred, if the thing can be arranged decently.

The Dowager Viscountess works hard at the match every season at Kissingen, even going so far as to pay her son's hotel-bills when he comes down by express train to have his addresses rejected every autumn. The Schochchild, however, though an airy creature not more than fifty-seven, is beginning to think that she must settle her 1200*l*. a year on herself, and marry somebody in time for the next coronation in France. Let us all hope she will select Timmins. They will be an innocent couple, and make quite a sensation in London if the Honourable Peregrine and his Baroness only spend their income on the right people. The capital of 1200*l*. a year must be at least 24,000*l*.; and that is enough to make a tolerable show for a time, if handled boldly.

Timmins need not care much about settlements, for lawyers can generally contrive to drive a coach-and-six through any marriage contract—that is to say, if the thing has not been done before. But there was an ugly story about in Vienna that made some people suppose the Schochchild might have paid the debts of a handsome Hungarian Baron Foray with every ducat she could raise upon her jointure; and such a mistake in finance, if it really happened, would be a sad disappointment to Timmins.

## VI.

### Attachés.

There was an extraordinary scene of rejoicing and excitement in Lord Mereworth's household on the day when my lady's favourite son, handsome Hugh Paladin, was first nominated for an attachéship in the diplomatic service of the Earl of Furby. Good luck seemed to follow the brave boy. He had been captain of the Oppidans at Eton, he had taken a double-first at Oxford, and yet was neither a prig nor a pedant, so that he had carried off a fellowship as easily and cheerily as Robert Cecil or Charles Murray. Now again he had been successful, and got a chance in public life for which many smart young fellows would give their ears, if wigs were still worn.

His father, Lord Mereworth, a peer of considerable influence, acknowledged with rather a sad look and hesitating manner, when cross-questioned by his wife, that he had been obliged to try all he knew before he could get the boy's appointment; and that Barker and Bullion-Huckster, the senior partner of a firm where he had been advised to open a deposit account with his Michaelmas rents, had really more to do with the success of his negotiations than either his old friend the Premier, or his brother-in-law, who was Lord Lieutenant of the county, and had gone up to Downing-street with him to push the thing. Nearly a score of peers too, all of whom liked Mereworth, had even mobbed Lord Furby for him at the Carlton.

Nothing, however, could be done till Barker was consulted, on the advice of old Truffleton. 'Then the business went easily enough,' added my lord dryly; and his wife could get nothing more out of him, nor did she try much, having already obtained all she wanted, and seeing that her Harry, good-natured as he was generally, had determined to go to sleep if pressed too closely. In truth my lord, who was of a kind and generous nature, did not like to take the gilt off his wife's fine new piece of gingerbread; and as she had made up her mind that the Mereworth family influence, when resolutely exerted, and backed up by all the county, could impose its own conditions on any Government, he thought it would be churlish to disturb a belief which was but another name for her love and pride of him.

Hugh's mere nomination for an attachéship did not quite settle his business as it would have done in

the gentlemanly old times. He had to pass rather a stiff examination, and to cram 'a general knowledge' of many things which were not true, and which would have been of no importance to any human being if they had been true. The publisher of 'Ker's Edition, 1862,' of an inaccurate book made something by this process; and so did several Whig printers of dull antiquated volumes; though Lord Furby was a Tory by trade.

Hugh Paladin scrambled through his examination as other hopeful and ambitious lads have done before him, looking on the whole thing as quite serious and respectable, poor boy; for he had been always a good deal at home, and the Mereworths, who were a God-fearing set, never suffered their children to drift away from fireside influences till my lady got that wretched diplomatic craze into her fond head.

Hugh was much changed, however, when he went down to Morlands, the ancestral place of his people, after six months' service on probation at the Foreign Office. He had been employed in the 'Hong-Kong Treaty Port' department, which was Dolly O'Carroll's room; and Dolly was better known as 'The Noble Cockahoop,' because he had injudiciously traced his descent to the Irish Kings on making his first appearance at the F. O. twenty years before, in a coat cut at Limerick, but which fitted him indifferently. Cockahoop, at first goaded to madness by taunts about his regal birth and conspicuous attire, had long since become one of the best dressed and most unassuming men in the department.

Hugh had hardly been three days in this excellent gentleman's room before he was inducted into all the mysteries of leap-frog, which happened to be the favourite game in the H. K. T. P. department just then;

and ere a single month was out the lad could sit soaking sherry and talking salt scandals with the best of them. The noble Cockahoop pronounced him to be 'a rattling good fellow,' which was the highest praise ever awarded to any officer in her Majesty's service, and was by no means lavishly bestowed. It is as satisfactory a form of laudation as any other; and what made it more gratifying to Hugh's feelings was the fact that every one, from the permanent Under-Secretary of State and the précis-writer down to Mrs. Housekeeper Mary Langcake, indorsed the noble Cockahoop's opinion.

Nevertheless, Lady Mereworth's sweet matronly eyes wore a look somewhat pained and startled when she saw her darling on Christmas-eve under the stately roof-tree of time-honoured Morlands. He had got on the most wonderful trousers ever seen; his hair, cut in the shoe-brush fashion lately imported from Paris, was not a quarter of an inch long; and the waxed points of his mustachioes stood out on each side of his face, as though he had just swallowed every bite of two gold mice, except their tails. The boy's handsome curly locks, which were a perpetual delight to her maternal soul, were all clipped away; and so, as the upper housemaid sorrowfully remarked, were 'his precious whiskers,' though my lord's own gentleman sulked with her for three

Sundays running at church, and would not read out of her prayer-book, because she mourned for them.

Hugh did not stay long with his kinsfolk on this occasion. He amazed them by some wonderful costumes, and broke out all over in a surfeit of strange jewelry. Lord Mereworth also observed, with much dry humour, on his advent at the cover-side in a complete suit of white fluff, which had made him look like a performing poodle, and had caused considerable hilarity among the members of the hunt.

'Indeed, sir!' replied the youthful diplomatist, eyeing his father with much coolness; 'poor things, your country families about here! I pity more than I condemn them. I wore the famous Compiègne uniform. The Empress calls it "Costume de Polichinelle voué à la Vierge." The noble Cockahoop, my respected chief, describes the illustrious sporting fraternity to which I have the honour to belong as the "Holy Iced-Punch Order."'

The impudent boy would have babbled on as flippantly during the whole of breakfast-time, but that Lord Mereworth's face looked so grave, and his mother said, 'O Hugh!' in rather a scared voice; for these worthy country folk, who seldom left their ancestral woods, had no taste for jokes about religion.

They could not find it in their hearts to scold their boy, however, though his manners chilled and shocked them a little; and my lord got up with a feeling of unusual sadness on the morning when the youngest of his sons was about to leave him. John, the heir, was with his regiment in Ireland; Harry was with the Mediterranean fleet; and Christopher, who was in the Church, never left his parish, for conscientious reasons; so that the old house would seem very dull when Hugh was gone also.

My lord went into his study, hung round with riding-whips and fishing-rods, and where several handsome gun-cases were piled one above the other for autumn service; and he began to whistle with a rueful countenance. Then he dashed something abruptly from one of his eyes, and took out his cheque-book.

'The boy will have to represent his country now and then,' mused Lord Mereworth sagaciously. 'He must have money, and the more he has the better. I can do without an establishment in London this year, and run up by express when there is a close division. I must ride old Dobbin too another season, though he is getting a little weak in that near fetlock joint.' Puff, puff; and my lord lit a cigar to muster up courage enough to write a draft in three figures, beginning with the Arabic numeral 5.

'God bless you, my child!' gasped Lady Mereworth hysterically, a few hours later on in the day, when the family travelling carriage was at the hall-door. 'God bless you, my child!' (kiss, kiss,) and then she nestled up to him and gave him her own prayer-book. 'Promise me always to say your prayers, Hugh,' added the noble lady, too proud to let a tear be seen, but weeping inwardly. Then she put the dear kind hand, which had been blessed by hundreds of the poor and helpless, into the breast-pocket of her son's coat, and left there all her savings. They amounted to just 200*l.* in new Bank of England notes—no more, for her ladyship conscientiously did her duty by her husband's dinners. 'There is one from me and—and—and one—from your sister Hester,' whispered my lady in her son's ear, taking her breath rather shortly, but still keeping up appearances with infinite bravery.

'Dearest, dearest Hugh! has mamma told you I won't "come out" till next year, so that you may eclipse the King and all his Court?' asked a glorious romp of seventeen, who hung on to his left arm, delighted at the sacrifice she had made for her grand brother.

'Time is up!' said my lord, looking at his watch, and making a sign to the outrider, who trotted forward to open the park-gates near a farm which had

HUGH PALADIN LEAVING HOME.

"She put the dear kind hand into the breast pocket of his coat and left there all her savings."

been lately enclosed. Then he thrust the watch into his son's hands, and pushed him into the carriage rather unceremoniously.

'Heaven and earth! what does the boy want with so many boxes?' observed my lord presently, to hide his emotion, when a turn in the road had hidden the carriage. 'A German valet, too, shaved as bald as a pumpkin! What next?'

His wife put her hand upon his mouth, that soft sweet hand which had so lately been busy in Hugh's breast-pocket; his daughter gave him a crisp little kiss on the nose; and thus stifled, silenced, and enchanted by his womenkind, the country gentleman returned to his usual avocations, and acquitted even a poacher almost without parley, he was so happy in the promises of greatness which the future held out to his son. 'Heaven grant that he may be an honour to his country,' said the stout baron to his wife as they went to rest that night. 'He is clever and honest, patient and aspiring, in spite of his light talk.'

'He will resemble his ancestor, Sir Frederick Beaufoye, who was at the Congress of Verona, and win an earldom for himself,' answered her ladyship, with perfect confidence.

'Ay,' continued my lord, taking quite the same view of the case; 'to be sure he will. I had never thought of that, my dear.'

So they fell asleep, and enjoyed some dreams of marvellous grandeur all lit up by Love and Hope.

Hugh Paladin was pleased with his place when he got there. He was not precisely 'treated as one of the family,' though the commission of an Attaché

LADY BADGER.

formerly enjoined his chief not ungracefully to give the lad something like a home when he first went away from his own people. Sir Bland Badger, his chief, however, who was an old Harrovian, took a fancy to him at once because he quoted Horace without ever making a false quantity; and Lady Badger really liked him because he brought her the first violets of the season, and he had learned from his mother the gentle word and knightly homage which please all worthy womanhood. He might have risen high in the service under able guidance, with such qualities as these. He was well born, well bred, not wanting in worldly knowledge. With but even a modicum of cash prudently invested, a pair of nimble heels, a happy knack of Latin quotation, and a classical master, he would almost certainly have advanced to the foremost and most responsible places in his profession.

But suddenly there was a hushed-up story about him, a story which was carried about in whispers by the Queen's messengers to all the hotels and coffee-houses in Europe. An august lady had been pleased to declare that the newest of the English attachés 'could sing like an angel;' for she had heard him, through the open window of his lodgings, exercising a mellow tenor upon the robber-song in Schiller's *Wallenstein:*

'Frisch auf Cameraden die Rappen gezaümt.'

It had been far better for Hugh if he had never learned German. Henceforth nothing would suit the august personage but that she and Hugh should sing all day long; and the lad's heart went out to her in his songs. No one ever knew whether her heart answered him; but she married another august personage, and drifted away from him evermore. Possibly Serene Highnesses have no hearts. He seemed lost, somehow, after the stately wedding in which he was obliged to take part officially. Thenceforth he became incurably addicted to high play and august company, though he could never muster more than 700*l.* a year, as all the world knew, including his fellowship and his mother's pin-money.

He lived an awful dun-hunted life for twenty years or more with his high-pacing ways and his heartache. His profession seemed to him such a trumpery thing, as, indeed, it was, when compared with what he had lost, that he threw it up, to wander after the fatal light which always led him farther and farther away into pathless marshes.

Thus one morning, not long ago, some gentlemen, who were reading the newspaper at their club, lazily noticed an announcement stating that when the leaves fall, there died 'at Monaco, on the 1st of October, the Honourable Hugh Paladin, fourth son of

Frank Fairfax, nineteenth Baron Mereworth.' Also, in another part of the same paper, was an advertisement intimating that 'unless the Honourable Hugh Paladin took away within three weeks from that date a brougham which he had left at Jobling's livery stables, it would be sold to pay expenses.'

'By the piper who played before Moses!' said

Lord Truffleton (the present Truffleton, who drives a sky-blue curricle), 'old Hugh died game. He went through life on wheels to the last. He had the best-appointed drag at Monaco.'

'Yes—*two*,' drawled Lord Protocol. 'The Empress Helena was at Cannes all the winter.' Having made this observation, his lordship glanced absently out of the window, which was a way he had when he thought he had made a point in the game of conversation.

# VII.
## Consuls-General.

There are several varieties of this particoloured species of public servant. But generally he is a disappointed man who has missed his tip; and who resembles neither fish, flesh, nor fowl, nor good red herring. The man who is Consul-General in Morocco, the man who is Consul-General at Yedo, and the man who is Consul-General at Teheran are exceptions to this rule, because they are also Ministers; and there are a few other gentlemen, known to the Foreign Office, who are alleged to be satisfied with their ambiguous condition in life for similar reasons. One of them goes about, indeed, under the odd title of 'Resident in the Persian Gulf,' which is enough to silence the murmurs of any mortal.

The British Consular Service is perhaps the only profession known among mankind in which a Secretary of State can, if so minded, abruptly raise his footman to a rank officially considered as equivalent to that of Rear-Admirals and Major-Generals, with far more than the pay usually enjoyed by these superior officers. The British Consular Service, as might be expected, has suffered accordingly. Persons of character and education do not like to be thrust against their will into offices, in which they may be superseded at any moment by a Maltese crimp—an event which happened frequently under the benign administration of Lord Furby; that eminently calm-minded Secretary of State having cautiously divided his best consular patronage between the honest class above mentioned, and any fine high-spirited fellows of his family taken haphazard, so that they were only in want of a salary.

Also many bright dreams and towering ambitions have lately ended in a consulate-general; because Lord Furby finds a natural pleasure in degrading the most eminent of the junior members of the diplomatic service, and they have either to take anything he throws to them, and to submit to his lordship's playful tricks with their emoluments, or to give up their professional livelihood altogether. Even a diplomatist does not like to starve in enforced idleness at forty or fifty years of age; and thus many doleful elderly faces may be seen issuing from the Foreign Office whenever Lord Furby returns to power in the usual course of British events parliamentary.

Those dejected old fellows were once men of mark and fair prospects, who, maybe, have served their country, not without distinction, at half a dozen capitals, from the petty Residenzstadt of some German kingling to Teheran, the most splendid Court of the East now left upstanding. Nevertheless Lord Furby has metamorphosed them by discreet methods into Consuls-General; and they would use their commissions as waste paper if they were not unable to keep up their life-assurances without a salary of some sort; after they have spent all their private property during some score years of deferred hope, ending thus. 'Ay, ending,' they growl bitterly, 'in abject dependence on the mercy of a light-fingered lunatic.'

There is another sort of Consul-General, though he is rather scarce. Herr von Geldermann and Baron von Schnapwitz, for instance, have a perfectly well-founded belief that the titular distinction of British Consul-General has a business value for them; and they profess this creed in common with reflective commercial men of all nations. They have a notion that their goods and persons would be protected by the British flag in case of civil wars or foreign invasion; and consular rank gives them not only a social position, but several important privileges mentioned in elaborate works by Miruss, Bynkershock, and other eminent writers on international law—privileges only encumbered by the condition that they shall be never used.

Finally, there is the orthodox old Consul-General, who was private secretary to Mr. De Mortmagne (of the great divorce case) from 1841 to 1845, and who has gradually writhed and crawled his way upwards till all his hair has come off with the exertion. He is still secretly frightened with the memories of it. This kind of Consul-General believes that his post in some African or South American mud village is the true centre of the universe. He is commonly a highly

respected old donkey, who walks about in the undress uniform of the consular service, with a formidable band of gold-lace round his cap. Thus accoutred, and inflated with the pride and pomp of office, he looks like the steward of a Channel mail-boat in a gale of wind; expecting that all within hail will do him obedience, as all may have need of his services.

His discourse in private life, and at its best, chiefly refers to the high price of vegetables, and to the changes which have occurred in the seasons since he was a boy. Sometimes, however, he dilates with extreme unction on the forgotten naughtinesses of a bygone generation; bringing forth the shadows of rakes and demireps from their unhonoured tombs, and seeming to like to tell how they drank and revelled, as though their poor grimaces and antiquated debauchery were the choicest part of history. This variety of Consul-General frequently wears a wig like the majestic wigs of George IV.; and rejoices with all his servile soul in the idea that he personally resembles the fat and heartless old King. His talk over his bottle, when in this vein of obstreperous loyalty, is not edifying; and a travelling clergyman is sometimes startled to hear his country's official representative volunteer to give imitations of the manner in which all the Royal Dukes were used to swear in the early part of the present century. In truth, the Consul-General was, perhaps, a notable character himself in a small way, and on the backstairs of fashionable life; so that he may have had many opportunities of hearing and seeing how the great of the earth disported themselves in the presence of their inferiors.

When he dies he will possibly bequeath about thirty thousand pounds, more or less, for probate duty, to some influential clerk in the Foreign Office; and also leave behind him a sealed packet of those explosive letters in the great divorce case to the Minister's sister, who was concerned in it. For those letters got him his place, and materially helped, with the influence of his heir the clerk, to keep it. There is a rude sense of dog-like fidelity to his old masters at the bottom of the vain old fellow's heart, after all; but he disowns his family because they are shoemakers at Brighton, and it is a heavy sorrow to him that he was not named after the late Bishop of Osnaburg of blessed memory.

## VIII.

### CONSULS.

Lord Palmerston, in his most offhand way, disposed of the social claims of Consuls when he told the House of Commons that they were '*not* gentlemen.' They are, indeed, the strangest set of people ever got together in the same profession. Large families of aliens are imported wholesale, from time to time, into the consular service; and not long ago an exceedingly disreputable company of persons, all closely related by birth or marriage, held every post on the sea-line of communication between Malta and Trebizond, extending therefrom again through Erzeroom to Tabreez and Teheran. In like manner, a family of attorneys, named Wilkins, did some quite amazing things with the British consular service in the United States of America. Nevertheless, the nobility is not altogether unrepresented in this branch of the public accounts. The family of one Scotch Earl alone have considerately taken possession of two consulates-general and two consulates, even carrying their patriotic condescension so far as to accept a vice-consulate.

As a rule, however, the consular service has

been wisely looked upon by successive Secretaries of State as a method of pensioning off those claimants and dependents, of both sexes, who have gradually gathered round them during an agitated political life. Intelligent couriers, the sons of valued stewards, valets, and cooks; convenient witnesses in perplexing law-suits; the husbands of enterprising ladies; with a free sprinkling of active-minded persons out at elbows and on the press, used to form the staple of the consular service.

The best sort of Consul still known is the retired naval officer, of the class often appointed formerly by Lord Aberdeen and his immediate successors. This Consul is a cheery, hospitable, straightforward old fellow, with stout bandy legs, good weather eye, and no nonsense about him. His consular salary and his half-pay as a Commander R.N. carry him cosily on to quarter-day in the style that he lives; for he does his marketing himself, and drinks nothing but cold grog without sugar. A very notable type of official is this rare species of Consul, and welcome as healthy weather in the house of every British subject throughout his district. He is still occasionally to be found in the Spanish seas and elsewhere; but has been almost elbowed out of the service, by Lord Furby's lot, since 1866.

One of the last of them was Jack Fowler, who

THE CONSULESS OF RHODES'S SONG.

I. 225.

married an English housemaid when he went home on leave for the last time, and lived in great dignity and honour ever afterwards. They had no children; but she was a great hand at a sea-pie when she had once learned to make it, and she taught her Greek cook to roast quails to perfection. Travellers who touched at Rhodes on their way to Jericho during this bonny housemaid's reign at her Majesty's consulate had many causes to rejoice; and she was one of them. A rosy-cheeked free-hearted lady, with a voice somewhat breezy and shrill, was this Consuless; but she did not rule too visibly over her husband and his guests when they were governable by unseen methods. It was her favourite practice to appear after dinner, when her housewifely duties were well ended, and sing a song of her childhood with exquisite archness and spirit. It began and ended, after many intermediate musical verses, something in this manner:

SONG OF THE CONSULESS AT RHODES.

'O foff! siz the straingur,
O foff! an daway,
An daway flew his lie dark
Till the silver of day.'

A pilgrim going to Jerusalem for the Greek Easter, and forced by stress of weather to put in at Rhodes, was so pleased with this melodious lyric, that he sought and obtained permission to copy it from the

Consuless's own dictation. Neither he nor she, however, was able to discover the language in which it had been composed, till the editor of *Notes and Queries* was referred to, and after deep study arrived at the conclusion that the text might be restored into that of a famous old English ballad.

Poor Jack Fowler's first fit was brought on by Lady Jemima Heyday turning up her nose at this song on a hot July evening. That lady and her husband thought it due to their dignity to be rude to their inferiors, because he was a Frankfort lottery-loan man, who had changed his name from Heideck on becoming a member of the British aristocracy, and she was the eldest daughter of a baron, who had often marched against his creditors into the impregnable fortresses of the Court of Bankruptcy. Jack might have recovered the blow to his consular dignity and uxorial tenderness; but a few days afterwards Lord Pedlington, the powerful banker, whose junior partner was First Lord of the Admiralty, sent off his scullion to buy 'a few coals of the Consul,' and evidently thought him a kind of bumboat man, nominated by Government for the special behoof of the Yacht Squadron.

Jack never held his head up after that, because he fell a good deal in the esteem of his buxom consort, the housemaid. She had previously considered her 'Cauensle,' as she proudly called him, the representative of our sovereign lady the Queen, seeing that he fired off a gun every day in his kitchen-garden before sitting down to dinner, which, she had been assured, was a Royal custom at meal-time. Now she felt that her self-esteem had had a fall.

She need not have been so down-hearted. There were Consuls, such as Rawlinson at Bagdad and Rose at Beyrout, who wielded more power than many kings. A man who held even a Vice-Consulate at Cos was seriously called 'Charlemagne' by his neighbours because of his loftiness. At Aleppo there was a Consul who dressed like a Turk, wore a long beard, and went by the tremendous name of 'The Supreme Being.' His father was one Bowker, who had done something wrong for a Duke of Cumberland.

Indeed, the good-natured Consuless of Rhodes got back some of her former respect for her husband's rank when she went on a visit to a Consul at Broussa, who marched every day to his roast mutton to the sound of martial music, played by his entire family, and solemnly served himself first at his own table in honour of his regal character. Jack, however, only murmured, 'Coals, Sarah Jane; only think of that! and the blanked landlubber sent us twenty Turkish piastres to pay for them, with a message that he did not want any change.'

Jack could not reconcile his dignity to that part of the story. He had never been offered a tip since he wore the Queen's uniform till he became a Consul; and he vowed he would have sent in his resignation, but that, on looking down the list of his colleagues, he saw the names of Burton, Playfair, Mansfield, Drummond-Hay, Churchill, and Sandwith, names which can only be mentioned with respect and honour.

LORD PEDLINGTON'S SCULLION COMES TO BUY A FEW COALS.

## IX.

### Vice-Consuls.

The commissions of Consul-General empower them to appoint Vice-Consuls, and their general instructions enjoin them to do so whenever there is a necessity for such appointments in the interests of British trade or shipping. In practice, however, they are never allowed to make such appointments; because a vice-consulate has been lately considered by the prudent and eminently judicious-minded Secretary of State who so long administered the Foreign Office as a thing of value, to be promptly snapped up and applied to his own use. A vice-consulate in honest hands indeed is a very small thing, being sometimes worth no more than 50*l.* a year, as at Toulon. Very often the post is not paid at all.

A sharp person, however, untroubled by scruples, can always make a cheerful occupation of it. He may graft on to it a flourishing business as a money-changer, an hotel-tout, a guide to the neighbouring antiquities, a ship-chandler, a sailors' lodging-house keeper. He can take part in various courageous and honest enterprises, which will seldom leave him with an empty pocket; for he can always make matters more or less unpleasant to seafaring men who object to deal with him. The commonest sort of Vice-Consul is therefore a keen-eyed agile creature, who is ever on the watch for small profits of all kinds, and who makes them with astonishing energy and perseverance, till he develops into a local notable, and contrives to get his son or his nephew appointed in his stead.

He can often lend money to the Consul, and therefore keeps his chief well under his thumb. He collects the fees and keeps the fee-books, takes charge of seamen's wages, so that all the pickings and perquisites of consular business fall to him. His intelligence is commonly composed in equal parts of shrewdness and greed. He may be recognised in most ports by the irrepressible gold-laced cap of his order, and by the suspicious looks of the shipmasters who speak to him on business. His method of dealing with their affairs, however, is more simple than one would suppose, and it is always the same. He merely gives them recommendations to the sea-lawyer, whose bills of costs he is ready to certify, and with whom he is privately in partnership.

The Vice-Consul's trade is a good one, because there is no check on the taxes extorted from ship-owners in our days. The sensible practice of making the Consul a notary, and holding him responsible for the fees he levied, was abolished at the instance of a late Assistant Under-Secretary of State, who had his own reasons for most of the things he did. The result is that British Consuls have now no interest in transacting the notarial business of shipmasters at reasonable prices fixed by law, and whenever they can they shirk having anything to do with it. The merchant-captain may thus be coolly handed over, with his cargo and ship, to a waterside rogue, who goes halves with the Vice-Consul in anything that can be either coaxed or bullied out of him.

It is quite refreshing to see the puzzled aspect of the master of a Newcastle collier, with the sharp Vice-Consul on one side of him and the sea-lawyer on the other. The shipmaster need not indeed trouble himself much about the matter. It is the shipowner who pays; and it sometimes happens that if Captain Drinkhard, of the Black-eyed Susan, has run up too large a bill for grog and smiles at the Vice-Consul's lodging-house, he can merge his account in the sea-lawyer's bill, and the Vice-Consul will certify that it is all right. The money can easily be raised by bottomry bonds, and all three are thus made happy.

The Consul or Consul-General, as the case may

THE PERPLEXED COLLIER CAPTAIN.

be, dare not complain of the lucrative transactions of his Vice-Consul. Just in accordance with the extent and success of them is the Vice-Consul certain to have potent friends among the attorneys and capitalists who manage Lord Furby, and do perpetual honour to that cool safe judgment and to that admirable statesmanship which has edified so many millions of newspaper readers in this great country.

There is also another species of Vice-Consul, who may be most accurately described as 'The Foreign-Office Dodger.' When a Secretary of State has notoriously had a relation of such a sort that his name is too well known to be submitted to the Queen for any important appointment, without a little circumlocution, that interesting individual may count upon a vice-consulate such as will not even bring him into hostile collision with the Civil Service Commissioners. He may reside at Dresden, at Naples, or at Rome, in short, anywhere he pleases, so that he does not come to England: and the Examiners will leave him at peace. He will also be exempted from any investigation into his capacities as soon as it is convenient to provide him with a Royal commission; and the Secretary of State may thus have things all his own way, under a snug Order in Council, dated June 4th, 1870.

Accordingly, the Foreign-Office Dodger who has a calm and judicious patron, such as Lord Furby, may be briskly moved from post to post without ever being required actually to perform any duty at all. Every move, however, will entitle him to an outfit, and his lordship gave no less than ten of these handsome gratuities to one fortunate fellow. By and by—all in good time, or before—say, for instance, in four or five years, varied by profitable incidents of travel—'the Foreign-Office Dodger' blooms brightly out upon the world as Envoy Extraordinary and Minister Plenipotentiary, with a salary of 4000*l.* a year—and a step or two in another profession, say the Army or Navy, just to keep our soldiers and sailors in good heart about the distribution of public honours and rewards.

Many neat things are done, too, in the special-service way, for this class of Vice-Consul; who is not so common as he should be, though there are several fine specimens of him just now in the service.

## X.

### QUEEN'S MESSENGERS.

One of the pleasantest trades going, thirty years ago, was that of a Queen's Messenger, and people who dealt in such things got as much as seven thousand pounds for the appointment. The salary of the place was rather vague, but its emoluments were considerable, and the Messengers travelled over Europe in well-appointed carriages of their own. Railways put a stop to this, and materially diminished, not only the profits, but the personal consequence of Queen's Messengers, who came henceforth to be confused with the crowd of ordinary first-class passengers by express trains. Then a more precise figure was made to represent their pay, and at last a reforming Secretary of State—who was, by the way, a Tory—abolished their perquisites.

Now Queen's Messengers are a humdrum company of orthodox persons. Some of the porters of the more distant embassies, however, could tell strange tales of their predecessors. One had such an exalted idea of his rank in life that, when Lord

Ponsonby's gatekeeper at Vienna came out at midnight in his night-gear to receive the Messenger's despatches, the Messenger chivied him half-naked down the street, for want of respect in not putting on his livery. Another Messenger, being stopped in Prussia for want of post-horses, rode forward upon a cow, till he met a Prussian officer, whom he knocked off his charger and took possession of it. He was forbidden ever again to put foot in the country; but was ultimately begged off punishment by diplomatic methods. All these honest gentlemen led exciting lives, full of adventure, and became general repositories of good stories and miscellaneous facts about all countries.

The crook in their lot was that the Foreign Office clerks crowed over them, and that, though they had a high opinion of themselves, their social position was not distinctly recognised. There seems to have been something shocking to the ears of gentlemen in the name of Messenger, though their duties, rightly considered, were scarcely beneath the attention of a rising statesman or an ambitious soldier. Men of rank and talent submitted without a murmur to be shelved in the pompous tedium of a petty Court; but a client of Grenville or of Fox would have felt insulted had it been proposed to him to obtain a practical view of the government and institutions of many countries, in an inferior position.

As Queen's Messengers are entitled to the promptest means of proceeding on their way, their baggage is exempt from search, and used in the good old times to be filled with international presents from great people. French bonnets, Brussels lace, and miscellaneous fashions choked their portmanteaus, carpetbags, and hat-cases, till there was a custom-house riot about one of them, who brought over sixteen thousand pounds' worth of shawls from Turkey for commercial purposes. Now a Queen's Messenger can only demand that the Government seal on his despatch-bags shall be respected. The rest of his luggage is open to inspection. Still a despatch-bag may be made to hold a good deal, and often does so.

As to the political use of Queen's Messengers, much may be said on both sides. They sometimes afford a convenient means of gaining time, when an Ambassador or his Government are in doubt as to the course they should take, and would like to see affairs ripen before they touch them again. In that case they are despatched with a general printing of paragraphs in evening papers, relating to the importance of their errand. At other times their bags are mostly full of love-letters, Foreign Office jokes, tradesmen's bills, and culinary delicacies.

To a cursory observer it has sometimes appeared that Ambassadors are more fond of fuss and importance than desirous to incur the expense of them; and in connection with this subject it has been remarked that, under Governments who pay their representatives a fixed allowance for couriers, most of the despatches sent by their Excellencies go through the common post. When the taste for mystery and hocus-pocus can be indulged free of cost to the Ambassador, he seems willing to gratify it; but when anything is to be gained by dispensing with these things, no more Messengers or special trains are required. Mystery in the abstract is, of course, a fine thing.

Perhaps it is also a profitable thing. A story got abroad, not long ago, of some mysterious gentlemen, who carried on a funny little game, in which Queen's Messengers, cipher despatches, and a foreign loan were all unaccountably mixed up together. A foreign State was about to repudiate its liabilities, and timely notice of the fact was thus opportunely brought to the knowledge of a favoured few. I am bound to say I have formed my own opinion of diplomatic mysteries in consequence of this and similar transactions ever growing more frequent. I apprehend that they sometimes supply a very lucrative business, and have a brisk sale. A lady has just made twenty thousand pounds by one diplomatic secret; and she has dealt regularly in them for many years. She is, of course, a fascinating lady. Some mysterious gentlemen are in correspondence with newspapers on remunerative terms, and sell the best items in the Messengers' bags by retail. There are quite a company of them thus engaged — a company, too, with very limited liability.

Another of the causes of diplomatic secrecy and sealed despatch-bags is that a whole set of people in authority are sometimes frightened and ashamed of the mess they have got into. The most touching little incident of this kind is a well-known European scandal, relating to a family of diplomatists who had *all* borrowed money of a certain stock-jobber. The secret affairs of their Embassy were most religiously kept. The riddle of the Sphinx, the secret rites of forgotten religions, were easy guessing to the wondrous things which might, could, or should have been concocted behind the impenetrable veil which shrouded the proceedings of these diplomatists. They had only confidence in one man on earth, and he was the stock-jobber. So a more thriving and mysterious set of fellows never blundered on together in the dark, made wild mischief, as was seen too late, and now sneer at all ill-conditioned people who presume to blame them.

I am sorry to refer to these circumstances; but the misfortune is that if one makes a general charge without particulars, an indignant army of expectant younger sons cry out, 'Where are your proofs?'

If you adduce plain, notorious, indisputable facts, the same set of exasperating dunces change their note, and exclaim, ' O, the libeller! O, the calumniator!' till well-meaning writers, who wish to point out a shocking abuse, really do not know how to state it so as to please them.

A curious illustration of the manner in which diplomatic secrets are kept occurred some years ago, under circumstances where no direct pecuniary interest is presumably in question. One morning a startling communication appeared in the *Daily News*, a paper with which I had been officially forbidden to have any connection. Nevertheless, the article was attributed to me by the Foreign Office, and my friends were aghast at the indignation expressed against me. To hustle me out of the service without even a preliminary inquiry was thought too mild a punishment, and as I had an active enemy among the upper clerks, a decree was passed that I should be 'crucified.' To crucify a man was the departmental word for badgering him till he was forced to resign his commission. I had, however, an ally in the enemy's camp, who told me what had happened, and that 'traps' were about to be set for me in consequence. Twenty-four hours afterwards I had the original draft of the *Daily News* article in my hands. It was written by the Ambassador's private secretary, with marginal notes by his Excellency, and it had been sent in the Messenger's bag. This document having been shown to the Secretary of State then in charge of Foreign Affairs, the case was hushed up, and I heard no more of it. I should hardly have got out of the scrape but for the Ambassador's imprudence; but he had a habit of carelessly tearing up his waste papers and tossing them into a basket, instead of fitting up a regular 'burning-room' for the purpose, such as they have at the F. O.

One word more about Queen's Messengers before this brief notice of them comes to an end. The bearer of important tidings is sometimes recompensed with immediate promotion, especially if he have suffered from danger and difficulty upon his journey; and an officer who brings home news of peace receives 500*l.* in accordance with immemorial custom. For English Queen's Messengers, and for them only, is neither reward nor promotion for good services, however arduous. Two have received no mark of official favour since 1843, one has been in the same position since 1852. Thirty-seven years of hard work gain no recognition whatever. Not a single Messenger now on the staff enjoys even an honorary distinction of any sort. A set of as fine, frank, enterprising, quick-witted gentlemen as ever wore boots are condemned all their lives to remain in a false and subordinate position; to be hectored by rude clerks, and to feel that the best directed energy and the most devoted attention to their duties are useless to them. A happy thought, which would make the professional fortune of a foreign officer employed on such a service, is sneered down or pigeon-holed in Downing-street with supercilious arrogance, and men who might be employed with singular advantage to the country are converted into mere postmen. Now we have certainly several gentlemen among our Queen's Messengers who possess great ability, and who are keen observers, whose experience, touching the state of countries through which they are constantly travelling, might be of great value in time of need. They are men of infinite resource, courage, and judgment, yet we obstinately refuse to credit them with any higher quality than a stout constitution, and leave their minds to grow sour with discontent. Once a Messenger, always a Messenger, whose attempt to rise higher is a theme for clerkly impertinence and dogged opposition.

## XI.

### INTERPRETERS.

Interpreters are now employed for the most part only in embassies out of Europe. Their duty is to translate official documents, and to interpret the conversation of their chiefs at official interviews. The Interpreters employed by the Turkish Government in their negotiations with Ambassadors accredited to the Porte were in former times usually functionaries of very high rank. They were nearly always Greeks, and they soon contrived to get the entire business of foreign affairs into their hands. It was from them that the hospodars of the rich provinces of Moldavia and Wallachia were almost constantly chosen. Since the outbreak of the Greek revolution, however, the Greeks have lost much of their power and influence at the Porte.

The duties of Interpreter require the utmost honesty and delicacy. The Porte was quite right in giving her Interpreters distinguished rank and emoluments. A sound negotiator is not always a clever linguist, and he must therefore employ somebody who is; that somebody must be thoroughly trustworthy, for he will often have it in his power to make or mar the objects of his chief. The Interpreters of the embassies at Constantinople have higher salaries than the secretaries of embassy and legation; still they are not beyond temptation; they do not form part of the Diplomatic Corps, as they ought to do; their position in society is not recognised; they are not looked upon as gentlemen. This is a very serious mistake, for they have literally all the business of the embassies in their hands; they are the official messengers between the Porte and the embassies; they are the real ambassadors; all depends on their tact, prudence, and ability.

On ordinary occasions it is useless for an Ambassador to make a long, solemn, pompous visit to a person who cannot understand a word he says. Therefore he sends a dragoman, who is received without fuss or ceremony; states his mission simply, without forms or absurdities, and sometimes gets a plain and satisfactory answer. I am afraid in my time there were not half a dozen dragomans who could interpret correctly the most trifling official document. The muddle into which affairs must get where they are singularly important and complicated, and yet are clearly understood by no party concerned, is better imagined than described. In short, the whole race of diplomatic interpreters are a weary lot, and it would only rouse an outcry to speak of them as they deserve. It would do no good whatever. Sir Alfred Sandison at Constantinople is doubtless a good Turkish scholar, and he is Oriental Secretary; but he cannot do all the business of the embassy; and I see the six student dragomans were all appointed on the same day (25th Oct. 1877).

Mr. Goschen must have got into odd perplexities with such a staff, and the Turkish authorities must have been quite unable to comprehend his language or his wishes. Lord Palmerston long ago wished to remedy this absurd state of things, and applied to the Vice-Chancellors of Oxford and Cambridge to recommend him the two most promising scholars they could find. Then this is what happened: the Dons both recommended their personal friends, looking upon the chance of doing so as a snug piece of patronage not to be thrown away. One of the persons recommended was a marquis, the other the son of a viscount, and both felt aggrieved that they were not considered as regular members of the Diplomatic Corps. Also they were left out in the cold too long, they received no promotion, and were seldom employed; so that they got sick of their business, and the whole scheme broke down.

Lord Stratford de Redcliffe habitually employed

Levantines, and quarrelled with them; but the Levantines were too much for him, and his pitched battle with his chief dragoman, Stephen Pisani, helped more than a little to upset him. Lord Dalling had his own ways of getting at facts, and knew the Turks well. Sir H. Layard, too, was not wholly without means of making himself understood. But if any one really wishes to know how and why the Eastern Question has got into such a hopeless muddle, he has only to ask himself what satisfactory outcome could possibly issue from the negotiations of people who habitually talk gibberish to each other.

## XII.

### AMBASSADRESSES.

The whole of an Ambassador's family, and especially his wife, are peculiarly under the protection of the State in which he resides. It is not, however, altogether correct to say that the family of an Ambassador share all the privileges of his rank and office; for his children and any relations who may reside with him are merely treated as foreigners of similar condition. The custom of Courts has, by degrees, made an exception in favour of an Ambassador's wife, to whom special honours are sometimes accorded; but even in her case they have been frequently disputed. Grotius, who was himself Ambassador to the punctilious Court of France, makes no mention whatever of the wives of Ambassadors, though he must have been well aware of any honours due to his wife, who accompanied him. The position of Ambassadors' wives, therefore, appears to be very much like that of the wives of Scotch Lords of Session, and James I. decided their legal rank. 'I,' observed the pedant King, in one of his lucid intervals between quoting Latin and slobbering his courtiers, 'made the carles lords, but who made the carlines ladies?'

In former times, he who was sent upon an embassy usually left his wife at home; but when, during the seventeenth century, permanent embassies came into fashion, Ambassadors' wives remonstrated with such energy and perseverance, that they were ever afterwards allowed to follow their husbands, and by all means to take their tongues with them. Then first was heard the title of Ambassadress, with which these ladies bedecked and ornamented themselves. Nevertheless, a French Envoy at the Hague, a profane single man, who had paid no attention to the important revolution going on in the diplomatic world, shrugged his bachelor shoulders at the arrival of a Spanish Ambassador's wife, and immediately wrote home to his Government, 'que c'était une Ambassade hermaphrodite,' a jest which delighted the French Court vastly.

Italy has the honour of having given a title to Ambassadors' wives; and Sixtus V. is the love of a Pope who confirmed it. The new dignity is said to have been invented as a peculiar mark of courtesy towards Count Olivarez (a judicious statesman who flourished under female rule), and who was then Spanish Ambassador at the Vatican. This Count, father of the still more famous Minister of Philip IV. (immortalised in *Gil Blas*), instantly seized upon the opportunity of giving a banquet to the Roman ladies; and it is needless to add, that Spanish interests at once became popular, for irresistible voices were advocating them all day long, and possibly part of the night, for ever afterwards during that generation.

The Pope was by no means a potentate accustomed to do things by halves. Having once conferred the title of Ambassadress upon the Countess Olivarez, he determined that she should forthwith enjoy all the advantages of her exalted rank. He permitted her to kiss his toe; and the nieces of all the Cardinals remarked, with pardonable envy, that his Holiness received her on this auspicious occasion with the ceremony due to a Royal Princess. Henceforth her rank was fully acknowledged, and she began immediately to quarrel for precedence with the princesses of Colonna and Orsini, so that no one could ever venture to invite them to the same house together.

Meantime it soon became apparent to the Pope that, since he had granted a brand-new handle to the name of the Spanish Ambassador's wife, he must concede the same advantages to the wives of other Ambassadors, or prepare to leave the Vatican, as the only means left him of escaping from their anger. To any person who has enjoyed favourable opportunities of becoming acquainted with the vigorous proceedings of a band of ladies, all of one mind on some particular subject affecting themselves, it will not be a matter of surprise that the Pope submitted without venturing upon a parley. He was painfully aware that negotiations must have added to his humiliation; and thenceforth the wives of all Ambassadors have held their own. Woe to those who do not religiously bow down before a title bestowed by a Pope and worn by a lady!

Pope Sixtus, however, was possibly unaware of the aspiring nature of the feminine soul, or it is a question whether he would not rather have endured an honourable martyrdom, to assure the peace of the world, rather than have taken such a step. He might have shut himself up in his palace, and excommunicated the turbulent females in his nightcap from an upper window. The thunders of the Church in those days struck terror into the hearts of the bravest. Perhaps they might have availed something against even a crowd of ladies; or, if he had held out till the last, and then died valiantly, he would have been entitled to the respect and affection of every usher and master of ceremonies in Europe.

Ambassadresses no sooner got their title recognised than they resolved to display it in full dress as publicly as possible. Quiet sober old fogeys, all tricks and wig, were promptly married by blooming and strong-minded young women of property and ambition. Widows of large fortune and a taste for society lay in wait for tottering elderly gentlemen who might have been their grandfathers, and led them off, in spite of senile struggles, to the nearest clergyman. There was quite a mania for Ambassadors among marriageable ladies. Numerous females who had long disappeared abruptly, in company with a jewel-case and a captain in the guards, turned up again in the most unexpected and distressing manner, to insist upon an instant restitution of their conjugal rights. Other energetic ladies, with false fronts and immaculate reputations, who had hitherto submitted to be stowed away in holes and corners, started off with great decision for foreign capitals; and Ambassadors, who were whispering sweet nothings in the interest of their country to the most celebrated beauties of Paris or Madrid, were startled by a well-remembered box on the ear and a peremptory order to take larger lodgings, from an awful creature in an antediluvian bonnet, whom they had not seen for twenty years. Diplomacy, from being rather a jolly profession than otherwise, became as dull as the private life of a comic actor; and most of the small-legged, knock-kneed, dried-up old beaux, in peach-blossom coats, who were among the diplomatic notabilities of those times, thought of the Pope with a feeling they were unable to express.

Moreover, the Ambassadresses appeared with such pomp and splendour at the first Congress held after their promotion, that no business could go on because of them. Their husbands were obliged to rise in the very smallest hours of the morning, and to meet by stealth, in order that they might consult upon some means by which the Papal plague could be mitigated. The French Ambassadress, of course, found them out, and at once raised the signal of revolt, while her husband turned traitor to the cause of his colleagues. Finally they got all they wanted, and the Congress separated without doing much worthy of record.

Among the Ambassadresses best known to us is the wife of Sir William Temple, who played a prominent part in State affairs during his momentous embassy to Holland. She negotiated a marriage which was destined to change the history of England —that between William of Orange and Princess Mary, daughter of James II. She carried on a long and very remarkable correspondence both with the King and the Duke of York, who had to be managed by very different methods. The wives of several members of the illustrious house of Temple have been among the stateliest flowers of English womanhood, and Lady Palmerston was not the least of them. The extraordinary career of Lady Hamilton, at the Court of Naples, shows what women can do and dare; and it is but folly to condemn one half the world as triflers for the friskiness of a few dames who love frolic too much. In our own time Madame Dosne, Princess Lieven, Princess Eliza Troubetzkoi have played a large part in politics; and Lady Waldegrave showed a fine clear wit when Queen of London. The Marchioness of Salisbury helped to mar her husband's work, both abroad and at home. The most gracious and best of all Ambassadresses, however, in this generation was the Countess Cowley. Her tact was innate, her mind active, and her manners absolutely perfect.

# SEMI-DETACHED WIVES.

# I.

## Introductory.

HE Semi-detached Wife is a lady whose husband exists, but not for her. He may be in prison, or mad, or playing the truant; he may be anything or anywhere; but he is not by her side, helping her to the best slices of his domestic bread-and-cheese, and giving her the cosiest place on his couch, as a tenderly attached husband should do. The Semi-detached Wife is an 'acting' widow, but without

widow's rank or privileges. She resembles those Scotch peers, who, not sitting in the House of Lords, are yet debarred from taking a seat in the Commons. Sometimes the Semi-detached widow owes her anomalous position to her own fault, sometimes to her husband's; but in either case the position is a trying one, and it is seldom that it can be held for long without loss of character.

There is a cogent reason for this; for all the world being deeply interested in the subject of matrimony, those ladies who have failed in their nuptial speculations find in every household a critic ready to ask why. To those who have succeeded, her failure may appear unintelligible; to those who have failed like herself, it may not always seem excusable, since there may have been in it some peculiarity which will cause others to think that her matrimonial lot was, after all, preferable to theirs.

There have been some famous Semi-detached Wives in history. Mesdames Shakespeare and Milton found it hard to get on with husbands whom all mankind admired; so did Lady Nelson and Lady Byron. Here we have four ladies wedded to heroes—four ladies whose lots must have seemed enviable to their respective contemporaries; and yet how much would they not have found to say on the other side of the question, if they had had any able counsel to hold a brief for them before the tribunal of history! The world has made up its mind that the four ladies named were wrong in their matrimonial squabbles; for it seems to tally with the general fitness of things that great men should have wives capable of comprehending them, and resolved to make them happy. But then great men are not always pleasant companions. They are apt to claim too much domestic worship, forgetting that home is a temple where wife should be the divinity. Let a great man be content with having his statue in bronze and marble on public market-places, but let him refrain from asking his family to erect him a pedestal beside his own hearth. Above all, let him not expect that the wife who is accustomed to see him in his nightcap will acquiesce in his continually adorning that homely headdress with laurels.

Women will give much reverence in exchange for a little love and tender treatment; but haughty patronage bores them. It is much to be feared that Shakespeare was by his own fireside a bore; Milton, with his mania for Greek and Latin studies, unquestionably was so; poor Byron suffered from an inflamed vanity which bled at the least touch; and Nelson was too fond of recounting to his lady the wondrous stories of his hairbreadth escapes by land and sea. At the seventy-seventh narrative of how gloriously the French were served one day in the Bay of Biscay the poor lady yawned, and no wonder. Nelson would have yawned too, if he had heard for the seventy-seventh time how her ladyship had worsted the baker's boy in a wrangle about accounts.

Thus much for historical Semi-detached Wives; and now may be introduced some specimens of the tribe who flourish in our midst at this present writing.

## II.

### AUTHORESS AND ACTRESS.

Everybody who is personally acquainted with the celebrities of the literary world has acknowledged the faithful likeness of the photograph of Mrs. M., which figures in most shop-windows. The attitude is slightly theatrical, and the expression of the features affected. The lady is standing near a desk covered with books; a huge hound crouches on a mat near her feet; she holds a quill-pen in her hand, and is gazing with enrapt interest at a sheet of paper, which the artist evidently intended to represent a page of manuscript, but which might just as well be last week's butcher's-bill. This is exactly as the popular novelist appears in real life, posturing for the admiration of her friends.

Her age is about thirty-five, and she had talent once, before she shredded it away by writing three sensational novels every year, to say nothing of magazine articles and essays on social subjects by the score. In proportion as her ability diminished, so, of course, did her vanity and intellectual petulancy increase. She railed at the critics, who had at first encouraged her with the utmost kindness, but who could not, without protesting, submit to the downpour of 'pot-boilers,' which her publishers had begun to rain on their heads. She shrugged her shoulders at remonstrance, and defied 'Grub-street' (as she humorously styled the critical band) to shake her popularity, yet with irritable inconsistency inveighed against the squeamishness of the public, who allowed the critics to warp their judgment. The truth is, that at the time when Mrs. M. had the photograph of herself and dog taken the public were beginning to feel as if they had had a surfeit of her novels. A story of murder, well told, in careful style and with an artistic grouping of characters and incidents, is entertaining enough; but some vulgar tale of crime or adultery, diluted in a thousand pages of wishy-washy prose, with characters as lifeless as barbers' blocks, and accessories having no more cohesion among themselves than the animalculæ which float about in a glass of Thames water—these are not a treat, but a weariness, to the reader. He can get his sensation much better and cheaper by reading the assize reports in a penny journal.

Mrs. M. had a husband, who was a clergyman; but it was believed that his wife's hysterico-bilious effusions had scared him into privacy, for he was

seldom to be met with. The two lived apart, though not judicially separated nor actually estranged from each other; and Mrs. M. often alluded to the retiring divine in a tone of half-contemptuous patronage, as if he were a poor wight, whom she had signally honoured by marrying. The reality was all the other way; for in the days when she was Miss X., the authoress had been glad and right proud to shelter her equivocal social position under the respected name of a scholar and gentleman; and poor Mr. M. had taken her to wife whilst her young fame was still in its bloom, and seemed to promise a magnificent flowering in future days. Mr. M.'s weak health, which rendered it advisable that he should live much by the seaside, was alleged as the reason why the couple did not reside under the same roof; but Mr. M. made such sparing references to his wife, even among those who knew him best, that persons often enjoyed his acquaintanceship for some time before they were led to discover his connection with the novelist, and curious mistakes resulted from this state of things.

One day, as he was travelling, a gentleman who sat opposite him in the railway carriage fell into conversation on literary matters, and the talk glided on to Mrs. M.'s novels, which the gentleman fervently abused. Mr. M. uttered lamentable moans, concurring in every word; but the gentleman's astonishment may be judged, when later in the day he met this sighing parson at Mrs. M.'s own house (the gentleman himself was a journalist), and was introduced to him as her husband. It was not often that Mr. M. put in an appearance at his wife's pretty villa at Norwood; and when he came the servants often failed to recognise him, and requested his card. His visits were generally on some charitable errand, such as begging Mrs. M. to contribute a little of her superfluity towards cases of exceptional destitution; and, to do her justice, she listened to such appeals the more readily as Mr. M. never asked anything for himself, seeing that he had a private maintenance of his own, which, though small, sufficed for his needs.

Sometimes it was Mrs. M. who would pay her husband a visit, swooping down, with maid, dog, and ten boxes, on the country parsonage, where he might be taking temporary duty for a friend. Perhaps she felt the necessity of occasionally placing herself *sous pavillon conjugal* for a few weeks, so as not to let the world lose sight of the fact that she had 'marriage lines' to show; but these visits flustered all the life out of Mr. M., for the authoress utilised them for the purpose of 'noting down types from Nature.' Seated in the rectory pew, with a loud bonnet on her head and a pair of gold-rimmed glasses raised to her eyes, she would stare about her during divine service, and thought it no breach of good taste suddenly to whip out a kind of betting-book, and jot down reflections suggested by some detail of architecture or the nasal intonations of the parish-clerk. On week-days she would patronise farmers and local gentry, asking odd questions, as if she were in a land of Caribbees, and everywhere proclaiming that she intended to lay the scene of her next novel in this part of the world; by which means she would cause a demand on Mudie's for at least three or four copies of her work more than would otherwise have been the case.

Generally speaking, however, Mrs. M. resided in her luxurious extravagantly furnished Norwood home, where she gave many semi-Bohemian parties, dignified by the name of 'artistic and intellectual *réunions.*' At these delightful gatherings it was the custom to say a great deal of good about Mrs. M.'s works, and a great deal of evil about those of other authoresses and authors not present. The hostess would gushingly explain the drift of her last and feeblest production, and the subtle sense of it, which had escaped the critics. Her tongue would clatter by the half-hour, as she expatiated on the high art of realism in literature, as illustrated by the minutely nauseous descriptions in which her pen revelled; and she would allude, with an affectation of deeply-contained energy, to the mighty novel which she *could* write, if she had to deal with a public freed from the uncultured hypocrisy which reigns in the British Isles. As Mrs. M.'s guests were not the leaders, but usually the sycophantic riffraff, of literature, they

AN INTELLECTUAL RÉUNION.
"She expatiated on the high art of realism in literature."

listened with well-feigned rapture to her verbiage, being at heart thankful for past favours, in the shape of succulent dinners, and hungrily anxious for a continuance of the same.

Touching the question of Mrs. M.'s morals, and whether she were chaste, or had ever been the contrary, or were likely to be, nobody in society cared two pins; but it was clearly her opinion that thousands of eyes were intent to watch whether she took any liberties with poor Mr. M.'s bright honour. The minds of women who live outside the pale of lawful conjugal restraints are habitually redolent of unclean suspicions. They sniff the air for unsavoury odours, and scent them from afar; they blush at words that mean nothing; they fidget with nameless impulses, and fancy that everybody can detect the signs of the guilty itch that torments them.

Mrs. M. gave you her inky fingers to squeeze in a sly way, as if this conventional mode of salutation might expose her to misinterpretation; she placed a forefinger on her lips at times and in places where there was no occasion for secrecy; she drove a French translator of her books half mad one night by fainting in his arms in her own garden, and assuring him afterwards that all London would be talking about it the next day. One of the favourite characters in her novels was the squealing female who is always ready for an elopement with the first male who comes to hand, be he baronet, groom, or music-master. But nobody, so far as we are aware, had ever proposed to elope with Mrs. M., or would have ventured upon such an unnecessary proceeding even to prove his love for a practical joke. She was an invincible fortress whom no man has assailed—a fruit which the fabulous fox would have called sour even if it had taken a header into his mouth.

Much better than Mrs. M., and the whole of that unsexed tribe who resemble her, do we love pretty, laughing, madcap Nelly N., the actress, who was in private life Mrs. P., though we believe her private life, so far as P. was concerned, consisted chiefly in telling him to go his ways, for that he and she had never been made for each other.

Why did not P. apply to the Divorce Court for release, seeing that he could have entered the witness-box with a sheaf of proofs under each arm, and a train of witnesses at his heels enough to fill Westminster Hall? Well, he loved his wayward, winsome, sweet-singing, naughty Nell, and never despaired that some day or other, when she had grown tired of breaking his heart, she would come back to him, who had forgiven her already times—almost seventy times seven. What made his infatuation the more ludicrously touching was that he had nothing in him that need have repelled an ordinary woman. He was neither a bully, rogue, or drunkard; but a respectable hard-working young surgeon, who had fallen in love with her one night when he had gone to the theatre with an order from a friend, and with whom she herself had been in love during six weeks or so—just time enough to marry him and repent of it.

She had a private house of her own, which had been furnished for her by a Duke, somewhere near Regent's Park, and poor P. often called there on a Sunday (in the forenoon, before visitors came), and appealed to her feelings. He wanted her to leave the stage, and promised that, if she would come home with him, he would toil eighteen hours a day that he might buy her the pretty dresses she was so fond of. Sometimes his despairing prayers moved her a little, and she would pass her hands through his hair, saying: 'Don't cry, Tom, poor old boy; I don't mean to be unkind, you know; but really we made a great mistake in marrying each other. I am such a wicked thing, that I don't deserve to be your wife; and if we lived together I should play you such pranks, that some day you would pitch me out of the window.'

Then she would laugh a little, and say that if he threw her out of the window he would be hanged for it, which would make her sorry ; and, amused at this view, she would laugh outright, till he joined in without ceasing to cry, for all his nerves were jarring. It was horribly pathetic; but Nellie was in the right, for poor P. was happier without her than he could have been in her society.

The fact is that she would not, or could not, keep straight. It was not that she had such an innate love of gay company, but gay company loved *her*, and had succeeded in turning her giddy little brain, which, in its calmest moments, had not much more steadiness than a weather-cock. The glare of the footlights, the songs she warbled so blithely, the enthusiastic applause of audiences had become as natural atmosphere to her; she felt as though stifled when removed from them; and all this had

brought its usual consequences of merry jinks in private life—dissipation, jewelry, champagne, lords, flirting critics, amorous brother actors, and other gay dogs galore. Why, bless her heart, Nell would pawn all her bracelets to carry an apron full of money to the widow of a scene-shifter who she had heard was dying of hunger; and one day she caught up a little starveling wench whom she saw selling violets, barefooted, in the streets, during a perishing March wind, and, carrying her off in her brougham, washed her, combed her, dressed her from head to foot in velvets and furs, and finally sent her home with two ten-pound notes in her purse.

All these things, and many others as impulsively kind, could Nellie N. do; but to be serious for ten minutes on any matter that concerned herself was not in her. Yet she could sing those pure old English ballads of love and faithful troth and homely joys with such accents as drew tears from the most hardened among the gilded crew who heard her; and on the stage she was most successful in enacting the characters of girls who are lovable for all the virtues of fidelity which she herself did not possess. Sometimes she would exclaim, with an instant's seriousness and conviction, 'If I were a man, and had such a wife as I am, I would strangle her!'

She had repeatedly offered her husband money to help him on in his profession; but he had, of course, refused, and she respected him for it. One day—a very bright day in spring—she alighted like a whirlwind at his lodgings, scampered up the stairs, and told him she had come to spend a long day—perhaps a whole week—with him. She laughed and cried, so did he; they lunched together, and were like bride and bridegroom again. But in the latter part of the afternoon Nell grew suddenly serious; then hurriedly put on her bonnet, and, after covering poor Tom with kisses, fled the house. She had been assailed by a passing fit of remorse; but it all vanished as she heard a barrel-organ playing one of her favourite airs, reminding her that it was impossible she could ever tear herself away from the stage, where her heart and life were.

One night Nell came away from the theatre with a headache; next day she was worse, and the symptoms of typhoid fever set in. She sent for her husband as soon as she felt delirium coming on; and he nursed her night and day through what was destined to be her first and last illness. If human skill could have saved her he would have done it; but the case was, from the first, hopeless. At the approach of death her consciousness returned for half an hour, and she recognised him, though he was wofully

altered. She sat up, with a vague glance in her large eyes, and asked abruptly,

## AUTHORESS AND ACTRESS. 275

'Tom dear, do you think they will burn me—for ever?'

'What an idea!' faltered wretched P., trying to induce her to lie down again.

'O, I know I deserve it,' she continued, shaking her head. 'But, Tom, I couldn't repent if I tried ever so much; and if my life were to begin over again, I am afraid I should act exactly as I have done. I was born wicked, you see, and it's in my nature; do you think *they*'ll take that into account?'

*They* did take it into account, we may be sure.

## III.

### Separated by Mutual Consent.

There is a category of Semi-detached Wives passably common in high life; namely, those who live under the same roof with their husbands, but have a separate establishment, do as they please, see whom they like, and only meet their lords at dinner-time or in society. These estrangements are usually managed so as to keep up appearances; and sometimes the disjoined parties contrive to remain very good friends, though they are friends, and nothing else. This, however, of course depends largely on the causes which produced the separation.

There are wives who voluntarily placed themselves in semi-detached condition because of an offence by their husbands; there are others who have been semi-detached to avoid the worse fate of a public scandal and divorce. In the former case matters often jog on fairly well; in the latter, the wife's condition is sometimes a shade or two worse than what we may believe purgatory to be. Yet this, again, depends much on the rank of the parties;

husbands of the highest rank being invariably the most forbearing.

All this is a question of money. Decorous estrangements are impossible among the middle and lower classes, because the parties cannot afford to carry them on commodiously. Fancy a husband and wife trying to remain punctiliously distant from each other in a set of six-room lodgings, or a mechanic living on terms of well-bred reserve with the wife who cooks his dinner. Among working people matrimonial squabbles are perforce settled by yells and blows; in the classes next above, who can screw together 100*l.* to buy a divorce, the parties rush off to Westminster, and pay lawyers to wash all their dirty linen in public.

Balzac has well remarked that it is only underbred persons who care to hunt after proofs of their own dishonour, and then trumpet them for the public amusement. Save under very exceptional circumstances, a nobleman would not thank the rascal who brought him tidings that my lady had forgotten her marriage-vow. He would much rather hush up so inconvenient a matter; and as for ladies of the aristocracy, they are, of course, obliged to evince the extremest indulgence touching the clandestine freaks of their husbands. Society would become a beargarden if gentlewomen made the same fuss as shopkeepers' wives every time their lords were convicted of flirting.

A delinquent husband of wealth and position, whose wife has put herself on semi-detached footing, has only himself to thank for a catastrophe which would never have occurred had he taken the commonest precautions to guard against his wife's dignity being wounded. In most of these cases the husband has acted so foolishly that it has been impossible for the wife to close her eyes to his escapade, and, being a proud woman, she has told him that she will never forgive it. She does not really mean this; if she could divine that her hasty words would cause her to live for years and years alienated from a man whom she has once loved, and perhaps loves still—nay, that death would part them before they had become reconciled—she would bite her tongue off sooner than doom herself to such pitiful loneliness.

But the words are pronounced in a moment of just anger; and the wealth of the parties gives them such facilities for effecting a quiet separation, that their new state of life soon becomes established as a custom which neither of them can well break through. They live in different parts of the house, seldom see each other except in the presence of servants or strangers, and on all occasions treat each other with a politeness which acts as a barrier to anything like cordial impulsiveness. Then the servants of the household, the relatives, and family friends, fall into the secret of the arrangement, and acquiesce in it as an accomplished fact; so that it would need a world of moral courage for either of the parties to venture on the first step towards a reconciliation, much as they both of them might secretly wish it.

Pride and false shame are terrible perpetuators of strife. A proud woman may fret over the past, but she will eat her heart out rather than let it be seen what she suffers; and, on his side, the husband, feeling himself in the wrong, and judging of his wife's sentiments by her cold mien, fears to risk advances which might be repelled to his discomfiture. Besides, in these estrangements, time operates against the wife, who, in growing older, sometimes loses much of her attractiveness; while the husband, being dependent for his means of solace, not on his good looks, but on his money, finds no difficulty in compensating himself for uxorial hostility after the Turkish and Mormon fashions.

It does not follow that a Semi-detached Wife glides at once into infidelity. There are women whose very pride keeps them pure in spite of all temptation. But if it should be otherwise, and if a woman should claim the same license as she sees her husband arrogate to himself as a right, the man only gets what he richly deserves. On this point let there be no sentimentalising, or sophistical talk about the difference between sexes. Nature has made the woman to be loved and cherished, and the husband's marriage-vow confesses her claim to his exclusive worship; but if the husband chooses to go and love and cherish other women, he must not be surprised if his wife regards herself as absolved from her own oath of faithfulness. Most husbands of aristocratic rank recognise this logic (pulling more or less wry faces as they do so); and their only stipulation is that my lady should not get herself talked about, or introduce into the family circle little boys and girls whom the putative father could not dandle with feelings of paternity.

Respecting Semi-detached Wives who have been offenders in the preliminaries that led to separation, it cannot be said that their lot is ever an enviable one. The most rakish of men has always a great deal to say about uxorial duty; and if he show himself merciful on grounds of policy, he will often consider it binding upon his dignity to treat his erring wife with a cold disdain far worse than the cruelty of downright abuse. Old men make terrible censors of young wives who have stumbled. Although their magnanimity may have proceeded solely from the

THE ERRING WIFE.

fear that they would cover themselves with ridicule by a publication of their connubial woes, they recur to their forgiveness with peevish iteration, until they either cow their wives into the condition of hysteric Magdalens, or drive them frantic into new exploits worse than the first. It is not every Robin Gray who can evince the equanimity of that old French duke, who, patting his young wife's hand, remarked pathetically: 'Ma chère amie, je me doutais bien que cela m'arriverait, mais pas si tôt.'

As a rule aged Frenchmen, Italians, and Spaniards are incomparably more adroit in making the best of a false position than Englishmen. They have more tact, good-humour, and philosophy; they shrink more sensitively from ridicule, and have a keener insight into the uselessness of lecturing a young and pretty woman who is bent on going her own way. One of these courtly old gentlemen, having been regaled by his own valet with reports of things unsuspected, slipped a bank-note into the rogue's hand, and said: 'Hush! don't speak so loud. Madame might hear you, and she would never forgive me.' Besides this, duelling enables continental husbands to avenge themselves in quiet summary ways that are not within reach of the British. Innumerable foreigners have been honourably pistolled at daybreak by veteran husbands, who had the good taste never to breathe a word to their young wives as to the motives which had led to these tragedies.

When a young husband ascertains things which every husband is the happier for never learning, the same philosophy cannot be expected of him as of an older man. In the first place the lady has, generally speaking, much less excuse for her misconduct; and if the husband be found condoning it, one may safely presume that he has reasons for so doing which redound little to his honour. Drunkards, scamps, and men afflicted with some bestial mania or other, are categories of men who do not care to face cross-questions in the Divorce Court; and there are other husbands who object to turn guilty wives out of doors, because they would turn out a great deal of money and many valuable connections at the same time.

These high-souled beings may be said to constitute the majority among the young husbands of Semi-detached Wives. They are tied by the tooth; they dare not raise a shout, because their mouths are full of the roast meats which their wives have stuffed there.

Say that young Mr. O. has married Miss Q., whose uncle John means to make her his heiress. Uncle John becomes the Providence and oracle of his niece's household. He pays the Christmas bills, sends hampers of game and wine, has always a spare 20*l.* note to satisfy Mrs. O.'s whims, and he helps on Mr. O. in his business or profession. If Mr. O. were to go to this old gentleman and inform him that his niece was a good-for-naught, he would be assisted down-stairs by a kick in the coat-tails, uncle John would take Mrs. O. to his home, and Mr. O. would be left to provide himself with meats and divorce-costs out of his own earnings. Mrs. O., who knows very well how the wind lies, has a gunpowdery way of exclaiming, on the slightest provocation, that if O. is not satisfied with her proceedings she will put on her bonnet and go; and the poor marital parasite is fain to vapour off his wrath in virtuous bluster which means nothing.

So little does Mrs. O. care for the spiritless fellow that she carries on her flirtations to his face. She goes to the theatre without asking his leave, wears jewelry which neither he nor uncle John ever paid for—though she will coolly tell uncle John in his presence that the trinkets are her husband's gifts—and she will receive afternoon visits from gentlemen of whose very names Mr. O. is ignorant, but whom he finds comfortably toasting their heels at his drawing-room fire when he returns from his office. One day Mrs. O. sends him a telegram announcing that she has been summoned to Brighton, and returns three days afterwards, saying she has been to see her aunt—she having no aunt. On another occasion O. receives an anonymous letter

SEPARATED BY MUTUAL CONSENT.
"Mrs. O. receives afternoon visits from gentlemen of whose very names her husband is ignorant."
I. 234.

filled with four pages of revelations as to his wife's amusements, and in nervous haste he pokes the dangerous communication into the fire. Next a cook, with whom Mrs. O. has had words about a missing joint, declares she will make a clean breast of everything she knows to 'master;' and master is obliged thereupon to put on a face of hot indignation, and order the hussy out of the house forthwith for daring to insult her mistress.

In the end things come to such a pass that O., who has long ceased to threaten that he will complain to uncle John, is in mortal dread lest uncle John should scent out something of his own self unaided. The sagacious relative has been seen to gaze upon his niece with a frown; he puts uneasy questions, and tells O. with a look that has somewhat of a searching expression in it that young wives like 'Jenny' require a good deal of supervision—all of which makes the dew of anguish ooze from O.'s brow. What if uncle John should bequeath his precious money away from his niece? The thought is so horrible that O. racks his brains for expedients by which the truth may be concealed. He becomes an active conniver in, as well as abettor of, his own shame; he invents the lies which his wife shall tell; he instructs her to show herself a little more affectionate towards him when the old man is looking on; and he himself drawls out such long yarns about his Jenny's domestic virtues that simple-hearted uncle John, who cannot suspect the depths of the cur's unclean villany, privately sets him down as the greatest fool who ever lived.

We repeat that husbands of Mr. O.'s type are not by any means rare; but if you called them dogs they might bring actions against you, and recover damages.

## IV.

### CANDIDATES FOR A DECREE NISI.

Some four years ago Mrs. S. came home from Madras along with her three children, leaving her husband behind in India. She cried a good deal at parting with the honest Captain, and he himself was equally affected, but the children's health required the separation. European children born in India generally begin to sicken about the fifth year; so it becomes a question with all British officials who cannot afford a summer residence for their little ones 'up the hills,' whether they shall lose their wives for a time, or their children for good and all.

There is the alternative of sending home the children alone to be educated by an aunt; but Mrs. S. was an affectionate mother, who did not wish her children to grow up out of her sight.

She went to live in London, taking a small house in a shabby suburban neighbourhood, for economy was an object. Captain S.'s income had been sufficient to keep his family comfortably in India, but it was hardly enough to maintain two establishments in the style which officers deem suitable to their rank. Mrs. S. soon began to regret her crowd of Indian servants, her flowery bungalow, the festive hospitalities of Madras, and that social queenship which all English ladies (and especially young ones) hold on Indian soil. The fogs and dirt of London, the dearness of all things, the sauciness and slatternliness of housemaids, and the lack of congenial society, told upon her spirits, and made her think that Fate had dealt hardly with her in condemning her to a life of genteel pauperism and virtual widowhood. Mrs. S. knew that five years, at least, must elapse before she could see her husband again, for it would have been unsafe to return with the children until they had been thoroughly seasoned by European climate; and the Captain himself could not afford the expense of six months' furlough and the journey simply to gra-. tify his affections.

Hundreds of Anglo-Indians stand in Mrs. S.'s position, and a very trying one it is. They are Semi-detached Wives, who, when they love their husbands, are profoundly wretched, and when they do not are very apt to treat their temporary freedom as if it were a definite one. They act like widows of the flightiest sort, frisk about to parties and places of amusement, run up bills, omit to pay them, or pay them with money never remitted from marital hands, until some bright day the husband—who has been privately warned by an officious friend or an anonymous letter—lands unexpectedly at Southampton, posts up to London without announcing his arrival, and discovers a variety of queer things, which are soon after revealed before a judge and jury, and become the occasion of a Decree Nisi, with costs against one or more co-respondents. It has been noticed that Anglo-Indian ladies form a large percentage of those who are cited before Sir James Hannen's tribunal.

Mrs. S. was too straight-minded a little woman, and moreover too fond of her children, to go wrong simply because she felt bored by her new position. But the depressing influence of London did undoubtedly develop some irritable propensities in her, and rendered her too pervious to sundry tales which began to reach her, anent her gallant husband's mode of comporting himself during her absence. Mrs. S. had made some acquaintances among the Anglo-Indian Londoners, and it was these who poisoned her peace, under pretence of conveying to her salutary warnings. They affected to pity her, and advised her to rebel. 'But what would you have me do?' she inquired piteously. 'Why, do as we all do —pay the men back in their own coin,' was the ready answer. Mrs. S. failed to see how such reprisals could console her for all she heard; and she felt very miserable to think that Jack S. was demeaning himself so unblushingly towards a certain odious Mrs. T., that 'all London' was gloating over his indiscretion.

Anglo-Indian ladies are continually receiving letters from the East, and circulate among one another all the gossip they contain, passing even the letters themselves on to their more intimate friends. In this way quite a fund of scandal reached Mrs. S. regarding her husband. Anglo-Indian ladies also receive many legates, in the form of officers or civil functionaries on furlough, who have been deputed by their husbands to bring them boxes of presents, such as shawls, ivory nicknacks, toys, and what not; and one bright day Mrs. S. was favoured with the visit of one of these emissaries, a middle-aged Civil Commissioner, with a beard two feet long, and a face like hardbake. Gallant withal, and talkative, this sunburnt placeman unfolded a fine quantity of Madras tattle, whilst he was helping Mrs. S. to unpack the trunk full of Hindostanish produce, which Jack S. had sent; and finally he unfolded the state of his own heart, which, said he, had burned with a pure flame for Mrs. S. ever since he had quadrilled with her at old Hookey's ball at Fort St. George, two years previously.

The avowal was not made in such blunt terms as

UNPLEASANT NEWS FROM THE EAST.

this; indeed it took several more visits before the full sense of it became manifest. But Mr. Commissioner Doubleyew was not a reticent mortal, and he made the best speed in pressing on to his point, which was, that Mrs. S.'s semi-detached status gave her an admirable chance of reciprocating in perfect safety the sentiments which bubbled within his own bosom, and the which, he was persuaded, would end by bursting their receptacle if she did not allow him to give them a free vent.

Mrs. S. was divided between the desire to turn Mr. Doubleyew out of doors with a broom, and the much more feminine impulse to lock herself up and have a good cry. She ordered the Commissioner never to show his face again; but he called the next day to beg pardon, and again, several days in succession, to make sure that her forgiveness was complete. There are men whom bolts and bars cannot keep out. The bearded Commissioner had a stock of effrontery which nothing could dash, and an inexhaustible vein of jocularity, which, while it rendered him irresistibly amusing, was well calculated to blind a female listener as to his real designs. Thus will the light skirmishers of an army, thrown out in front of a line of battle, conceal the movements of the forces manœuvring behind. Men, who know how to make a lonely woman laugh, are always dangerous.

However, Mrs. S. was dangerous herself—as a beautiful and well-armed citadel. Mr. Commissioner Doubleyew, who had set out a-conquering, was outflanked in his siege operations, driven off his guns, and finally made captive, with arms and baggage. And the besieged won this victory with little trouble.

There sprang up between the two an attachment, which was violently passionate on his side, and coolly calculating on hers. She liked the man without loving him: he was kind to her children, obedient to her own slightest behests, a man of affluent circumstances and good professional prospects, who was probably on the high road to a K.C.B.-ship—just the person, in fact, to make her an excellent second husband, in case she should decide upon divorcing Jack S. Mr. Commissioner Doubleyew's friends told him he was making a fool of himself; but he did not think there lay any folly, or even unmanliness, in urging a delightful woman to separate herself from a fellow who was cutting capers three thousand miles off, and evidently did not care for her a straw. He intrigued among the Anglo-Indian ladies, so that they should din into Mrs. S.'s ears incessant tales of the Captain's jinks, and drive her to exasperation by their cackling sympathy. He himself worked with hypocritical cleverness by pretending to disbelieve the awkward stories; and he could not be got to

admit that certain bits of scandal published by the Madras papers, and which sorely troubled Mrs. S.'s peace of mind, could only refer to Captain S. All this, however, simply made Mrs. S. feel the more certain that, out of regard for her, he was hiding a great deal of what he knew.

She felt a bitter resentment against her husband for having exposed her to these indignities; and when, at last, she told the Commissioner that she would play the tame victim no longer, she seemed to hint that she relied upon his good offices to assist her in all the legal steps necessary to procure her release. This task Mr. Doubleyew accepted forthwith. A couple of discharged servants recently returned from Madras—the one a lady's-maid, the other a drunken butler; a slanderous major, who had a personal grudge against Captain S.; and two or three other loquacious persons, whose belief in the Captain's guilt was based mainly on hearsay reports, furnished a mass of evidence which, submitted to those able lawyers Messrs. Ferrit & Pry, made up a first-rate brief to put into the hands of the eloquent Serjeant Bumpus.

One vital element was, however, wanting to make Mrs. S.'s case flawless, and that was the allegation of cruelty. No cruelty, no divorce, is the law as regards the weak sex. Mr. Pry begged the petitioner to sift her recollections, and earnestly consider whether there had never been a slap on the face, a tweak of the ears, or 'just a little pinch on the arm before witnesses, you know,' which could be magnified into gross inhumanity; but, rack her memory as she might, Mrs. S. could not remember that Jack S.

had ever affronted her with so much as a harsh word. This was unfortunate, and it remained for the Captain, by giving his wife a swinging box on the ears, to perfect a case which was in other respects beautifully complete.

The unfortunate officer had for some time past been struck by a tone of discontent and covert insinuation which pervaded his wife's letters, and also by the curtness of these epistles. He answered in a style of affectionate banter, thinking he had only to deal with that jealousy which is a proof of love, and comes pretty naturally to all young women who are separated from their husbands; but one morning there fell upon his breakfast-table, like a bombshell, a letter full of blots, tears, and wild reproaches, ending with the distraught intimation that the writer had confided her interests to persons who were willing and able to protect her. The next mail brought a communication from Messrs. Ferrit & Pry, who begged to be informed of the name of Captain S.'s solicitors, on whom they might serve a citation.

All this was absolute ruin to the Captain, who found himself obliged to borrow money at high interest to return to England and prove his guiltlessness of a charge which he considered mere trumpery, and which really was so. He was compelled to mortgage his commission, to renounce a chance of professional advancement which opportunely presented itself at this moment, to sell off horses and divers other belongings at a loss, and to fritter away 100*l.* in a series of telegrams, costing 5*l.* each. However, he could not disculpate himself by electricity; so home he came, indignant, raging, and persuaded that his wife must have lost her reason.

Perhaps a temperate explanation between the parties might have set matters right, for Jack S. loved his wife better than any woman on earth; he doted on his children too; and Mrs. S. herself was not yet so hardened but that the charm of his presence, coupled with a judicious display of kindness and repentance on his part, might have moved her to tears and forgiveness. But angry people go to work in the wrong way, and the Captain, forgetting that he was on his defence in the matter of Mrs. S., chose to take umbrage at the assiduities of Mr. Commissioner Doubleyew, of which it would seem that some little bird had reported to him more than enough. He taxed his wife with levity, heartlessness, dereliction from all her duties as a mother; and the result was a scene of vituperative recrimination and sobbing, which drew up the servants to the keyhole, and was finally brought to a climax by the Captain's calling his wife a simpleton, and dealing her such a slap on the cheek as resounded through the passage, and thence carried joyful echoes into the office of Messrs. Ferrit & Pry, Pump-court, Middle Temple.

There was nothing for it then but to go to work hammer and tongs. The Captain's lawyers retained Mr. Rumpus, Q.C., and filed a counter-petition against the wife and Mr. Commissioner Doubleyew as co-respondent. A day was set down for the hearing; and Bumpus and Rumpus came into court, with freshly powdered wigs, to do their best in a cause which promised plenty of fun.

SERJEANT BUMPUS.

Who that has ever attended one of those ignoble Divorce-Court suits has been able to refrain from sincerely pitying the parties to it? That women of the sort who bring actions for breach of promise—that brazen-faced jades, tipsy trollops, and women who have been bullied to the verge of idiotcy—should carry the confessions of their infamy or unendurable wretchedness to this rowdy tribunal is comprehensible; but that a woman having any vestige of modesty or dignified good sense should do so is only explicable under the supposition that she has no idea of what she is going to face. Long before her own counsel, Bumpus, had finished opening her case, Mrs. S. felt ready to sink through the floor from shame. Loud-whispering women in the galleries stared at her through opera-glasses; the barristers' benches

ogled her; and the spectators crowding behind greeted every one of Bumpus's humorous pauses with prolonged titters. The judge indulged in an occasional smile, and never ceased to take notes.

But after Bumpus it was the turn of Rumpus to lift up his voice; and then came the witnesses, mumbling, prevaricating, nervous, and red, till the laughter of the court gave them a moment of ribald boldness, soon to be checked, however, by the torture of cross-questioning, which caused them to writhe and spit out lie after lie. Then it was that Mrs. S., burying her crimson face in her hands, felt as though the wide earth could never afford her a spot dark enough to hide in. Some of the abominable accusations that were levelled against her by Rumpus made her stagger and gasp, as if the bewigged rough were flailing at her with a whip. And then those witnesses, what a crew!

Suborned menials, who had peeped through chinks; foul-minded old women, 'who had pieced two and two together;' cabmen, who swore to having driven Mrs. S. to places she had never visited; hotel-waiters and chambermaids, who thought they could identify her as the lady who had occupied

'No. 26' with a gentleman; a baker's boy, who had seen a man, the very image of Mr. Doubleyew, issue from her house at early morning; and Private Inquiry agents, who had lumped all these testimonies into a concrete of nastiness;—these were the persons who were subpœnaed to prove that Jack S.'s wife had behaved herself with the Commissioner as the vilest of the vile.

RUMPUS, Q.C.

'Aha, gentlemen of the jury,' bawled Mr. Rumpus, 'the plaintiff is, you see, a pretty sort of person to come into court with a story of pretended wrongs. Now that we have unmasked her, I look with confidence to your verdict being in accordance with her deserts.'

After this burst of rhetoric Mrs. S. fainted, and had to be carried out of court.

But British judges are shrewd men as well as learned; and he who presided in the Divorce Court, having winnowed the chaff of evidence from the grain, pointed out that there was not enough of the latter to feed even a scandal magpie. The jury, without leaving their box, returned a verdict that both parties had failed to substantiate their allegations; in other words, that both the Captain and Mrs. S. were stainless; whereupon the judge paternally expressed a hope that the combative couple would contrive to make it up.

Make it up, indeed! Just as if people who had spent a whole day in bespattering each other with mud would feel an inclination to rush into each other's arms and kiss! Mrs. S. might have forgiven Captain Jack for his abandoned doings with Mrs. T., but to her dying day she could never forget how he had inhumanely sat by while Rumpus was belabouring her; and the Captain, on his side, though he might have overlooked the draining expenses to which he had been put, and the utter ruin of Mrs. T.'s reputation, which had been caused by his wife's fault, could never pardon 'that blackguard Bumpus' for having so savagely vilified him by her orders.

If it had not been for their soreness at the deplorable handling they had both undergone in court, the pair would have rushed off to Westminster and had a new tussle about the custody of their children; as it was, they agreed, through their solicitors, to fee an eminent barrister 100*l.* to arbitrate on this point. The Captain declared he would never suffer his wife to keep the children after the outrageous way in which she had behaved; and so the arbiter decreed that the three little ones should be confided to a relative, where their mother should be allowed to visit them under restrictions as to time and frequency. Captain S. of course undertook to bear the costs of the arrangement, and to allow his wife so much a year for her own maintenance. These things being settled, the Captain returned to India. As for Mr. Doubleyew, he likewise went back to his commissionership, but contrived to keep out of his enemy's way, having been emphatically cautioned that if he came within reach of him, he would be made to dance a jig to the music of a horsewhip.

Moral of the foregoing little story: Mrs. S. will remain an unhappy Semi-detached Wife so long as she and her husband are both alive.

## V.

### A VERY VIRTUOUS SEMI-DETACHED WIFE.

The Countess Z. may or may not have been *née* Matilda Thompson, but there is a rumour to this effect which prevents her coronet from being regarded with the reverence usually bestowed on such august symbols. When an ex-governess claims to enter the spheres of nobility it is desirable that she should walk in on the arm of the husband who has ennobled her. Yet this the Countess has never been enabled to do. Count Z. is alive, and flourishes with all the vigour of a Polish magnate, who has managed to save a comfortable income out of the wreck of his down-trodden country's fortunes, but he and his wife live apart. Why?

Count Z. resides chiefly on continental race-courses; and when greeted with an inquiry as to his wife's health, he gazes at the tips of his boots, and brings all his scattered wits to bear on the question as to when he last heard from the faithful partner of his pecuniary means, then looks up with a troubled expression, and answers, 'She is very well, I think, thank you,' and shambles off as if he were being poked fun at. The Countess is not quite so reticent on the conjugal topic, for she is often heard to remark that she expects the Count home 'every day;' but the days roll themselves into months and years, and still the Count never appears to rejoice in the affectionate preparations which, we may conclude, are made every morning to receive him.

There is a little mystery at the bottom of this situation which will, perhaps, bear looking into.

Count Z. is not the *premier venu*. He has dabbled in war and politics; been a general of insurgent troops, a conspirator, member of a provisional government, and, at odd moments, a pamphleteer of no mean talent. At Warsaw, in 1863, he held the Russians in check till brute numbers gave them the victory; his compatriots adore him; and his head is worth ever so many roubles on the Czar's territory at this moment.

After the quenching of the Polish rebellion Count Z., wounded and sick at heart, came to recruit his health in England, where he was received with the distinction usually accorded to foreign revolutionists, though it is, for some inexplicable reason, denied to those of indigenous growth. He became the guest of a philo-Polish peer, and this peer's children had a governess, who, like my lord, felt enthusiastically towards barricade heroes in general,

COUNT Z. AND THE BROTHERS THOMPSON.

and towards Count Z. in particular. The Count soon won her heart, gave her a bracelet in exchange, and thought he might cry quits on those terms. But Miss Thompson was a better hand at a bargain.

She had three athletic brothers, who waited on Count Z., and declared to him that if he did not repair the breach he had occasioned in their sister's honour, they would make such an example of him that he would start thenceforth at his own shadow. They hastened to add, that they would listen to no foreigneering nonsense about duelling with sword or pistols. If he hesitated to marry Miss Thompson they would prosecute him for breach of promise of marriage; and after that, dog him from city to city, and chastise him in public places. The eldest of the three pulled out his watch, and gave Count Z. fifteen minutes to make up his mind.

Now the revolutionary chief was a little man, but valour does not depend on inches, and he was as brave as a well-plucked weazel. If he had had to face a simple question of dealing with three troublesome Thompsons, he would have flown to the poker, and cracked their three pates before they had had time to notice which brother had been hit first. But Count Z. was in heart and soul a gentleman, and most sedulous to preserve unsullied the reputation he had acquired as a soldier, patriot, and Liberal. He considered that the whole Polish cause would be involved in any dishonour that befell him personally; and Heaven knows that Poland had but too much cause to bewail the unworthiness of many a son who ought to have set a blameless example in exile.

In a cold and rapid way, judging his own case, the Count saw that he had offended, and that there were no excuses for him. Had he not abused the hospitality of Lord X., by trifling with a governess under his own roof? had he not trifled with the miserable girl herself, by dazzling her with his fame and assumed love (Count Z., though brave, was not too modest)? and had he not given these three puddle-blooded Englishmen the right to say that a Count Z. had acted as a liar and a rogue? What would all honourable-minded Poles say if these things were published in the newspapers? What would his countrymen of Warsaw think if they saw the Russian officers commenting on his case with jeers, as they read it aloud in the *cafés?* and what would his brother Liberals of the secret societies do if they learned that he, the advocate of equality and popular principles, had declined to marry a poor girl whom he had ruined, simply because she was not his equal in birth?

The upshot of these dismal musings was that Count Z. begged of the three Thompsons the hand of their sister. He did not yield to craven fear, but purely to the exigencies of his position as a man of honour and a noble. And the marriage took place accordingly, in the Polish church of London.

This, however, was but the first act of the matrimonial comedy. When the wedding was over the happy party adjourned to an hotel, and there Count Z. made his wife a little speech in the presence of her brothers. He said: 'Madame, you have fallen in love with my name and fortune, and now they are both yours. The latter within proper limits you may dispose of as you please; but the former I require you to keep free from blemish. I shall not live with you, for our characters would ill agree; but if it ever reaches me that you have done anything calculated to bring my name into dishonour, I shall come to your house, *and I shall shoot you!*'

Then turning to the three Thompsons: 'And you, gentlemen, be pleased to remember that as your sister is my wife you have become my relations, and I expect you to behave yourselves in such wise that I shall never have to blush for you. I hope this hint will suffice; for you can ascertain by inquiries among my friends that I am not a man to be trifled with. I have done my duty; now do yours.' The three Thompsons felt a momentary inclination to smile, in the consciousness of their unassailability as

Britons, but something in the look of Count Z.'s steel-blue eyes checked this process of exhilaration. Possibly they all three wished at that minute that they had left their sister to take care of herself.

Count Z. went off to France, and abandoned him-

self to turf pursuits—not as a blackleg, but as a gentleman. He was fond of horseflesh; and having nothing else to do, now that his *mésalliance* had debarred him from domestic joys, he set up a racing-stable, trained his horses himself, and ran them with considerable success for the best prizes. His colours have always been highly respected on the turf, because it is known that the nags who carry them run 'straight.'

The Countess Z. remained in England, and began to lead a life of compulsory virtue, the like of which was never devised before for the enslavement and worry of a Semi-detached Wife. Being a romantic person, she soon had romance enough for her needs in the circumstances and surroundings of her extraordinary existence; an existence of gilded fetters, under close espionage, and with a vision of death's-heads to haunt her by day and night.

Her husband had refused to introduce her into London society, not wishing his wife to be laughed at for her low origin or deficient manners by the gentlemen among whom a Countess Z. ought to have trod on a footing of equality; and he would not allow her to reside abroad, because she might easily have fallen there amongst other Semi-detached Wives of doubtful repute. As she was an Englishwoman, her proper place was in England. If she were to go on the Continent, and he lived apart from her, people might be asking questions.

He had given her four Polish servants, who were devoted to him, with the same kind of fidelity as Scottish clansmen displayed of yore towards their chiefs. The eldest—a lady whose husband was in Siberia, and who had herself been rescued from butchery at the hand of Russian soldiers by Count Z.'s bravery—acted as her housekeeper and, when the Countess desired it, as her companion; a younger woman, the Count's foster-sister, was her maid; and a pair of male Poles, Dobelwitz and Trikski, who would have cut each other's throats, or any one else's, at a sign from their master, whom they had served in the wars, filled the posts of coachman and butler. These servants had orders to treat their mistress with the humblest deference; to obey her in all things; but to keep incessant watch over her actions. The groom, footman, cook, and housemaids were English, but had been carefully chosen for their respectability by the housekeeper, Madame Marieneff, who spoke our language almost faultlessly.

At first the ex-Miss Thompson found her luxurious existence pleasant enough. She had 4000*l.* a year (a third of her husband's income), a fine house in Belgravia, her carriage, and a box at the Opera; and it amused her to show herself in parks and thea-

tres, richly apparelled and attended. No hindrance was placed in the way of her going to the seaside or visiting her relatives in the country; and she was free to receive at her own house what friends she liked, provided only they were persons of unimpeachable character. She gathered round her some of her former pupils who had married; a few clergymen's and doctors' wives; some ladies with whom she became acquainted in serving as patroness on charitable

committees; and sundry friends of her family who had known her in childhood; altogether a decent and presentable circle, which would have satisfied any woman content to lead a quiet life that none could carp at.

But the ex-Miss Thompson was not fashioned to appreciate the blessings of humdrum respectability. The instincts of virtue were not in her, nor the cravings after paths of peace. It humiliated her to be the only Countess in her circle. She would have liked to awe her clergymen's wives and family friends with throngs of sister countesses and baronesses, till their souls grew sick with envy, and they learned to feel how great an honour she, Countess Z., was doing them in receiving them at her board. One summer, at Scarborough, she fell in with an authentic Polish Princess, as affable as she was rich and pretty, and the pair became inseparable friends in the course of a forenoon; but as soon as Count Z. received news of the intimacy he wrote one of his laconic notes: 'Princess V. is not a suitable friend for a lady of your rank; she is an adventuress, and I request you to drop her;' and drop her Miss Thompson accordingly did, gnashing her teeth.

Her next move was the essentially feminine one of seeing whether she could not induce her husband to remember those idyllic days under Lord X.'s roof, and make him fall in love with her again. The bar to this was that Count Z. had never really been in love with her; but of this she was not aware. After all she was a well-favoured wench, with magnificent hair and shoulders, who looked mighty well in cerise or violet, and still better when she sat for her photograph in black silk, and with a pensive expression, intended to convey profundity of poetic thought. She had read Tennyson and the Lakists, and, like most other governesses, could dash off a grammatical love-letter, loaded with quotations, points of admiration, scraps of philosophy (from Tupper), and passages underlined. Of these she indited not a few, for her husband's behoof, on mauve paper, emblazoned with coronet and escutcheon. At first the Count returned curt answers to them; but finding they still continued he lit his cigars with them, unread.

Stung to the quick at his silence, the ex-Miss Thompson thought she would play yet one more card, and, moved thereto partly by a melodramatic episode she had witnessed at some theatre, determined to rush off to Paris, surprise her husband, and throw herself into his arms. But she had forgotten the telegraph. Long before she had crossed the Channel the Count, apprised by Madame Marieneff, had betaken himself into seclusion; and on alighting at the Gare du Nord the Countess was greeted by one of her husband's friends, a polite and elderly Polish Prince, who had been deputed to express the Count's regret that urgent business had called him into the country, but who respectfully placed himself at the Countess's orders, to show her the wonders of the French capital.

After a week's weary sight-seeing, and drives in the Bois, under the escort of this courteous but always impassive grandee, Countess Z. returned to England, with rage and vengeance shooting fiery throbs through her veins.

Her first step on reaching London was to call on a solicitor of Gray's Inn, and inquire whether British law furnished no remedy for a grievance so anomalous as hers. The solicitor replied that she might certainly plead for a restitution of conjugal rights, and, if she could acquire proofs that her husband was acting unfaithfully to her abroad, she might apply for a divorce on the ground of desertion, &c. But the lawyer felt obliged to add that Count Z. being a foreigner, British courts of law would have little hold upon him. He might snap his fingers at citations; withdraw the handsome allowance he was making her; and if sentenced, after a divorce, to pay alimony, might refuse to do so, and throw the whole costs of the action on herself. Was her ladyship prepared to run these risks? asked the solicitor. Her ladyship looked uncomfortable; on second thoughts it was obviously wiser to rest on her 4000*l.* a year and be thankful.

However, the solicitor had imparted to the ex-governess one grain of comfort, in that he had pooh-poohed Count Z.'s menaces about shooting. She had been moved to tell him that she stood in danger of her life if she did but speak a word of civility to a strange gentleman; and the lawyer had answered that, God be praised, there was yet a gallows-tree in Newgate—forgetting too readily, perhaps, as lawyers are apt to do, that if Count Z. were suspended by the neck, this fact, though reassuring to society at large, might not bring all the compensation desirable to his wife in her coffin.

Nevertheless, Miss Thompson took heart of grace, and, feeling herself under the protection of the hangman, resolved that, since the abject appeals of love had had no effect on her husband's heart, she would try what a little jealousy could do. She set off to pay a visit to Mr. Thompson, her father, taking only her maid with her, and without loss of time embarked in a violent flirtation with a visitor at his house, young Mr. Smith, an officer of the Line. One night young Mr. Smith was picked up in a country road, beaten to a jelly, and with his nose in a puddle. When restored to his wits he stated that a pair of garrotters had waylaid him; but the police asked how he could reconcile this version with the fact that he had lost neither watch nor money.

COUNTESS Z. AND YOUNG MR. SMITH.

It subsequently reached the Countess's ears, by mere accident, that during the whole time of her sojourn in her father's house her two servants, Dobelwitz and Trikski, whom she believed to be in London, had been residing in the neighbouring town, not three miles from her. There was nothing to implicate them in the discomfiture of Lieutenant Smith, and she was reduced on this point to bare conjecture. But she owned to herself, with an inward shudder, that her feet stood, in truth, on slippery places, and that it behoved her to mind how she walked.

More than twelve years have now elapsed since Miss Thompson married the hero of Warsaw, and from first to last she has never made a slip. Madame Marieneff and the Poles still keep house for her, and between them all she leads the sort of life to which princesses of the blood and ladies of feeble intellect are subjected. Her enforced propriety has earned her a good name, however, and not a few admiring friends, who may suspect that there is some mystery at the bottom of her life, but know not what. She gives parties, and allays suspicions by remarking that she is expecting the Count home from day to day. She points to letters lying on the table, and alludes to some piece of information which they are supposed to contain, observing that the

Count is an indefatigable and charming correspondent. She also professes—poor woman!—to have seen him 'six weeks ago,' or 'last season,' at Brighton or St. Leonards, and to have spent 'a delightful month' with him, though the real truth is that she has not once looked on his face since her wedding-day.

The Count's political proclivities being well known, he is always reported to be engaged in preparing a movement against Russia; and the Countess adroitly plays her part as a good wife, intrusted with all her husband's secrets, by expressing Russophobian sentiments virulent to the intensest degree. In pursuit of this same plan she subscribes to all funds for the relief of sick and wounded Turks, in her husband's name as well as her own. She confesses an attachment to the Hungarian cause, pities the French and Danes, has a bust of Garibaldi in her drawing-room, and finds a good many warm things to say in behalf of all revolutionists and exiles. It is a dismal comedy she plays, but it must be owned she plays it well; and if she harbours—as it may well be supposed she does—sentiments of the most unquenchable hatred against all foreigners in general, and especially against Poles, she wisely keeps them locked up in that innermost corner of her heart, where men and women do best to confine those impulses which it would serve them nothing to lay bare.

## VI.

### Ulysses and Penelope.

The gilded miseries of Countess Z. have their counterpart, but under a mitigated form, in the life of Penelope, wife of that charming but always absent soldier, Major Ulysses Gallivant, of the Staff. Penelope was a good wife at first, and adored Ulysses, till the latter grew tired of her fondling and sent her home to England, under the pretext that the climate of Malta, where he then resided, was not good for her. Evidently the fogs of London were preferable. Gallivant himself, however, throve well in any climate where there were fair women and snug bachelor quarters. The man loved his ease. Marriage, after the few years' trial he had given it, seemed fraught with considerable drawbacks, not the least of which was that when his wife was present Gallivant could not flirt to the top of his bent. He had a queer conscience, full of loopholes and turnings, and he had ended by persuading himself somehow that, since women may become such potent allies to a man in his career, it would be good for his wife as well as for himself that he should flirt. He would have argued in the same way as to the necessity for his getting regularly drunk, had he cared for drink. As it was, he often took champagne 'for his stomach's sake,' saying to himself that, as bread-winner of his little household, it was his duty above all things to sustain his health with good cheer. But he thought small-beer was good enough for Penelope.

Ulysses Gallivant was an arrant liar. He lied chiefly because he loved flattery, and must needs for ever be relating adventures in which he had taken a chief part, or explaining big schemes by which he proposed to do wonders for himself, Penelope, and the little ones. His adventures were mostly invented, and his schemes all came to nothing; but it was years before Penelope grew tired of hoping in him, and detected his incorrigible mania for fibbing. Lying is the one art in which men do not come to excel by constant practice. On the contrary, lying, to be long successful, should be practised sparingly, and never without reason. Gallivant could not do the simplest thing without enshrouding it with mystery, and telling lies to explain this mysteriousness. So it came to pass that every letter which he sent home to his wife was full of the most wondrous falsehoods as to what he was going to do, and why he did it. He was going east; perhaps he should be ordered west. He had become the confidant of his General; the most bril-

liant honours were awaiting him; he would be home with his wife at Easter, quite certainly—not later; or he was pining for a sight of her, and could not endure separation any longer. All this simply amounted to saying that U. G., who had promised to be home at Christmas, wanted to join a pleasant party who were going to leave Calcutta to winter in the Hills. At Easter, Gallivant had to join unexpectedly in an expedition to the frontier; and at midsummer he was ordered with despatches to Cairo. Up the Nile, down the Nile, in the field of battle, in the hunting-field, here, there, everywhere, Gallivant was always coming home, and never came.

This went on for years, and Penelope in her London lodgings had to make a decent show of continually expecting the truant to return. But women grow tired of waiting, and Penelope, who was fair, had suitors. *Tant pis* for Gallivant. The childish fibs which he blew homewards, like inflated toy-balloons, very round and highly coloured, ceased at length to be novel or amusing. Gas, gas, *toujours gas*, is apt to tire. Penelope could not let her youth be wasted in joyless languor. So long as she kept up appearances, she would assuredly be doing her duty quite as well as Ulysses did his; and if he were not satisfied, why, he might come home.

He has not come, and will probably not do so, till some day, disease and disaster falling upon him, he will return to spend the remainder of a peevish querulous old age at the fireside of the wife whom he deserted. Then he will require nursing, and Penelope will have the joyful occupation of putting hot flannels on his back and feeding him with cough lozenges. One day he will have a fit, but recover; then another, but get well again. Penelope will have to waste all her last stock of good looks in tending  him through his final struggles with death; till at length, when her release comes, and she dons her widow's cap, she will see tell-tale gray hairs frizzing out underneath it. The poor woman's liberty will have come too late. After living for years a husbandless wife, she will have to die a husbandless widow; for of course those suitors who crowded round her whilst Ulysses was away will have taken to flight on his return. Penelope's is a sad story; but then Ulysses was a sad dog, and there are, unhappily, many like him.

END OF VOL. I.

www.ingramcontent.com/pod-product-compliance
Lightning Source LLC
Chambersburg PA
CBHW020303240426

43673CB00039B/687